P9-DXM-829

WHISKEY
TANGO
FOXTROT
THE REAL LANGUAGE OF THE
MODERN AMERICAN MILITARY

WITHDRAWN

WHISKEY TANGO FOXTROT

THE REAL LANGUAGE OF THE MODERN AMERICAN MILITARY

ALAN AXELROD

Skyhorse Publishing

Copyright © 2013 by Alan Axelrod

All rights reserved. No part of this book may be reproduced in any manner without the express written consent of the publisher, except in the case of brief excerpts in critical reviews or articles. All inquiries should be addressed to Skyhorse Publishing, 307 West 36th Street, 11th Floor, New York, NY 10018.

Skyhorse Publishing books may be purchased in bulk at special discounts for sales promotion, corporate gifts, fund-raising, or educational purposes. Special editions can also be created to specifications. For details, contact the Special Sales Department, Skyhorse Publishing, 307 West 36th Street, 11th Floor, New York, NY 10018 or info@skyhorsepublishing.com.

Skyhorse® and Skyhorse Publishing® are registered trademarks of Skyhorse Publishing, Inc.®, a Delaware corporation.

Visit our website at www.skyhorsepublishing.com.

10 9 8 7 6 5 4 3 2 1

Library of Congress Cataloging-in-Publication Data

Axelrod, Alan, 1952-
 Whiskey tango foxtrot : the real language of the modern American military / Alan Axelrod.
     pages cm
 ISBN 978-1-62087-647-3 (pbk. : alk. paper)
1. Soldiers--United States--Language--Dictionaries. 2. Sailors--United States--Language--Dictionaries. 3. English language--United States--Slang--Dictionaries. 4. Military art and science--United States--Dictionaries. I. Title. II. Title: WTF, the real language of the modern American military. III. Title: real language of the modern American military.
 PE3727.S7A95 2013
 427'.973088355--dc23

                        2013011431

Printed in the United States of America

For Anita and Ian

TABLE OF CONTENTS

★ ★ ★

Book (1), Slang, Military

Geneticeneral George S. Patton Jr. once observed that, next to war, all other human endeavors pale into puny insignificance. Actually, it might have been George C. Scott playing Patton in the 1970 biopic directed by Franklin Schaffner. Doesn't matter. For one thing, Scott played Patton better than Patton ever played Patton, and, for another, the statement is pretty nearly true no matter who said it. For what is more costly, in money, materials, effort, pain, and life, than war? What requires a greater degree of coordinated energy? What else so tasks the hearts and minds of so many? What other human endeavor encompasses such a range of undertaking, from acts of deepest secrecy and darkest crime to the grandest mobilization of entire peoples, with vast armies shaping and reshaping the world?

And what else produces so many words, acronyms, and utterances than fighting wars and preparing to fight wars?

There is no grander or humbler stage for the enactment of language than war. War leaves untouched no aspect of human activity and emotion. Words born of the profession of arms describe the most exceptional, extreme, exalted, daring, and horrifying deeds as well as the most mundane: laboring, eating, eliminating, washing, cooking, fornicating, sleeping.

Over many years, soldiers, sailors, marines, and airmen have built their own language to express everything from the raw emotion to the complex technology in the lives of a group of professionals whose vocation is to kill people, break things, and, afterward, come home alive. They labor in a trade freighted at the highest levels of politics and command with words intended as much to conceal and deceive as to reveal and illuminate. At the lower level—the level of the **eleven bang-bang**, the ordinary seaman, the grunt **gyrene**, and the **balls-to-the-wall** pilot—it is a job just as focused on seeing through and cutting through the nonmeaning and nonsense emanating from the **Five-Sided Squirrel Cage** (i.e., the Pentagon).

The sources for the words and phrases in this book include such "official" authorities as the *Department of Defense Dictionary of Military Terms* (www.dtic.mil/doctrine/dod_dictionary/) and S. F. Tomajczyk's magnificent *Dictionary of the Modern United States Military* (Jefferson, NC: McFarland, 1996), but the most compelling elements of military language have no "official" sources. They come from the bottom up. *Whiskey Tango Foxtrot: The Real Language of the Modern American Military* is devoted to the linguistic world of that lower level, a world alternately hot, cold, horrible, glorious, squalid, adrenaline-charged, worked to exhaustion, lifted by comradeship, desolated by loneliness, and bored to desperation, a world in which words must be as sharp as bayonets.

The military is both a distinctive way of life and a community, and a command of what we might call the community's "folk speech"—its slang—is essential for admission to full membership within the group. Some military folk speech is familiar almost exclusively to the troops. A **shit screen**, for example, is a fall guy, the person who takes the blame for some foul-up or infraction. A **jarhead** is an enlisted marine. Other elements of military vocabulary, as you will see, have become part of our general folk speech, military and civilian. In both its exclusively military and more general military-civilian forms, the "real language of the modern American military" embodies a uniquely American attitude and an exuberantly colloquial, unwaveringly honest, and enduringly American grace under pressure.

ONE

Behind the Butt Plate

Living the GI Life

★

1ˢᵗ CivDiv

Mythical military formation Marines join when they leave the Corps and reenter civilian life: "1st Civilian Division."

A-Farts

Ad hoc acronym for American Forces Radio and Television Service, which broadcasts to U.S. armed forces—in camps, on ships, everywhere—worldwide.

Anymouse

On board U.S. Navy ships, the name for the lockbox in which sailors are welcome to drop *anonymous* suggestions.

Army Crimes

What GIs call *Army Times,* the official weekly periodical published by the army "for their benefit." Alternatively, the publication is known as ***Army Slimes***.

Asshole buddy

One's best, most trusted friend, comrade, and confidant. There is no sexual connotation whatsoever. **Asshole buddy** is a prime example of a dysphemism, the polar opposite of euphemism. Whereas euphemism pretties up an ugly situation or concept with a mild word—"independent thinker" to describe an obstinate moron—dysphemism uglies up a desirable situation or concept with an unpleasant word. This is typical usage of language in the rank-and-file American military.

Attaboy

A reward given to an individual soldier, sailor, airman, or marine or to an entire unit for a job well done. The reward in question might be nothing more than a word of praise from the commanding officer, a weekend pass, or a special treat at mess. Cynical commanders often use the expression **petting the animals** as an alternative to **attaboy**.

Baboon ass

Rumor has it that the U.S. Navy serves the finest cuisine of any military in the world. Sailors who've eaten USN corned beef, a staple they call **baboon ass** in the service, will tell you otherwise.

Bag of smashed asshole

Used to describe (generally to his face) a soldier whose uniform is sloppy, dirty, wrinkled, or in some other way grossly unsatisfactory. "Private Pyle, you look like a **bag of smashed asshole**." By extension, the phrase is sometimes applied to anything—a building, a vehicle, a weapon, a piece of machinery—that is damaged or worn out.

Balls

Beyond the obvious, this is a term for midnight as it appears on a twenty-four-hour digital clock: 0000. "I'm on post from **balls** to ten."

Bare-ass

Universal GI pronunciation of *barracks*. "See you in the **bare-ass**, Sarge."

Barney Clark

In a U.S. Navy shipboard mess, a slider (small hamburger) topped with a fried egg. ("Gimme a couple of those Barney Clarks!") The etymology of the phrase is obscure in the extreme. Barney Clark (1921–1983) was a retired dentist who received a permanent pneumatic total artificial heart designed by Dr. Robert Jarvik and implanted on December 2, 1982, by cardiac surgeon Dr. William DeVries. When implanted, the most advanced and familiar version of the Jarvik heart—the Jarvik 7—created a prominent circular bulge under the skin of the chest, apparently suggesting to the vivid imagination of hungry sailors the shape of the egg-topped slider.

Behind the butt plate

What a grunt just back from the front lines traditionally answered when asked where he'd been. The *butt plate* is a metal or rubber strip that reinforces the butt of a rifle stock. If you're behind it, the rifle is in front of you, with its business end pointed toward the enemy.

Bends and motherfuckers

Squat thrusts done by recruits during PT (physical training). The routine is this: stand, squat, place hands on ground, thrust feet back, do a push-up, return to squat, return to stand—and repeat until the DI (drill instructor) is exhausted (from yelling).

Bib

The rectangular piece of cloth that hangs from the back of the neck of the uniform of the U.S. Navy enlisted sailor is called a **bib**. This is not intended as a slur, but dates to the era of wood and sails, when ordinary seamen generally wore their hair long, braiding it and dipping it in tar (used to treat rigging and to seal planks on ship) to keep it from getting caught in block, tackle, and other rigging machinery. When given liberty ashore, a sailor would fashion a "bib" from sackcloth and tie it around his neck to keep the tar off his shirt. The practice became so universal that U.S. Navy command adopted the **bib** as an official feature of the regulation uniform.

Big PX in the Sky, the

Tongue-in-cheek evocation of heaven. "PX" stands for Post Exchange, an on-base store in which many of life's little luxuries can be bought more or less on the cheap. This phrase is related to, but must not be confused with, **Land of the Big PX**, a synonym for the United States, typically used by service members stationed far from home.

Blue Dick, the

Personification of the U.S. Navy. "Two weeks in port and no liberty! **The Blue Dick** strikes again."

BOHICA

U.S. Navy acronym signifying B*end Over,* H*ere* I*t* C*omes* A*gain* and used when a highly disagreeable order, assignment, outcome, or situation unsurprisingly recurs. Seaman Doe: "What? *Another* day of rust-scraping detail!" Seaman Joe: "**BOHICA!**"

Brain housing group

U.S. Air Force pilot's pseudo-technical term for the human skull.

Brown Shoe

Coined in World War II, when U.S. Navy aviators and submariners wore khaki uniforms with brown cordovan leather shoes, the term continues to be verbal shorthand for those personnel. In contrast, a **Black Shoe** is any U.S. Navy sailor or officer who does not serve on a sub or fly an airplane (and who, back in World War II, would therefore have worn a navy blue uniform with black oxfords).

Bucket of steam

Something seasoned sailors send raw U.S. Navy recruits (and sometimes brand-new ensigns) to fetch on their maiden voyage. This is similar to the order to "**Fire a polka-dot flare!**"

Bumfuck, Egypt

Generic name for any undesirable duty station in the U.S. Navy.

Bush hanky

Press the side of the nose with a finger, bend over, blow hard, and you have a **bush hanky**: a technique for expelling mucus without the use of a handkerchief (because you have none), your sleeve, or a bandana. The product of a **bush hanky** is known as a **bush oyster.**

Button chopper

GI laundry detergent, which, apparently, is scientifically formulated to dissolve clothing, buttons and all. "Throw some more of that **button chopper** in the wash, would you? I got inspection tomorrow morning."

Cadillac

Sooner or later, every sailor swabs a deck. The unlucky ones are given a bucket and a mop. The lucky ones are issued a **Cadillac**—a bucket on wheels and equipped with a wringer for that mop. Alternative meaning: The principal form of transport for a United States Marine, "Cadillac" is an old nickname for USMC-issued infantry boots.

Canned pork chops

What marines call beer.

Chicken shit

As applied to military life and routine, **chicken shit** is anything essentially inconsequential that is given exaggerated importance. Soldiers who served in General

George S. Patton Jr.'s II Corps in Africa, Seventh Army in Sicily, and Third Army on the Continent complained that the general's insistence on wearing regulation-knotted neckties, regulation leggings, shined shoes or boots, and helmets was not just **chicken shit**, but **elephant shit**, which is merely a huge amount of **chicken shit**.

Cover

In the U.S. Navy and Marine Corps, the term applied to any cap or hat.

Crack house

Most areas aboard U.S. Navy ships are "smoke-free zones," and smoking sailors are confined to designated enclosed areas that quickly fill with a dense nicotine haze. These miasmatic dens are shipboard **crack houses**.

Crotch, The

What marines call "The Corps" when they're in a really bad mood.

Crusher

The U.S. Army Air Forces flat service cap as worn in World War II. Fliers found the cap's visor highly useful, but they removed the stiffener that gave the top of the hat its flat surface so that they could wear their headsets (headphones) over the hat. The result was a distinctive fashion statement that was widely admired by women and envied by members of nonflying service branches.

DA Form 1

"Department of the Army Form 1," the civilian name for which is toilet paper.

Day the Eagle shits, the

Payday. As understood by soldier and civilian alike, "the Eagle" personifies the United States government. In civilian company, a soldier might substitute *screams* for the earthier word.

Dead horse

In the days of sail, enlisted sailors were often short on cash and could apply for an advance on their pay. This done, they were obliged to work off the period of time covered by that advance. The period was referred to as **dead horse**, and the act of working during this period was called **beating a dead horse**. The variant expression, **flogging a dead horse**, was first reported in 1867, when the British member of Parliament John Bright remarked that trying to nudge a conservative Parliament from its noninterest in the democratizing Reform Act of 1867 was like trying to "flog a dead horse" to make it pull a load. The *Oxford English Dictionary* reports the first printed occurrence in an 1872 newspaper article. This said, John Stephen Farmer and William Ernest Henley, in *Slang and its Analogues Past and Present* (privately printed in 1891), reported that **dead horse**, meaning work performed for pay in advance, was in use by the seventeenth century, and they cited as proof this sentence from a work called *Nicker Nicked,* published in 1669: "Sir Humphrey Foster had lost the greatest part of his estate, and then (playing, as it is said, for a dead horse) did, by happy fortune, recover it." Farmer and Henley also noted that, in the Royal Navy, seamen, "on signing articles" (beginning an enlistment), sometimes received an advance on pay, celebrating "the term of the period thus paid for by dragging a canvas horse, stuffed with straw, round the deck and dropping him into the sea amidst cheers."

Death From Within

U.S. Army airborne (paratoop and helicopter) units use the motto "Death From Above" to describe what they deliver to the enemy. Throughout the rest of the army, however, the motto has been changed to describe what military chow delivers to a GI's GI tract: **Death From Within**.

Deep six

Outmoded navy term for heaving something overboard—"deep six" being the lowest fathom (1 fathom = 6 feet) above the ocean floor. Today, a sailor discarding something into the ocean is more likely to report that he or she is just doing a **float** (or **flotation**) **check**.

Dickbeaters

Army slang for *fingers,* which are found attached to **dickskinners** (*hands*) and which should never be put in one's **dicktrap** (*mouth*).

DILLIGAFF

A highly euphonious acronym that poses the rhetorical question, *Does It Look Like I Give A Flying Fuck?*

Dixie cup

The familiar white sailor cap worn by enlisted U.S. Navy sailors through the rank of petty officer first class.

Dogsbody

Any sailor assigned an especially menial task. The origin of the term is found in the age of wooden ships, when British sailors applied the word to describe such staple rations as soaked sea biscuits and pease pudding.

Double-digit midget

An extreme short-timer—a service member with fewer than 100 days before his or her hitch is up or before he or she rotates out of a combat area and gets back to "the world."

Double-O

Examine very, very closely. "Lieutenant, give this report the **double-O** before you send it to the colonel." Some authorities believe the expression is an initialism for O*nce* O*ver*, but because it means a *close* examination, it is most likely a reference to a person's two eyes.

Dynamited chicken

Navy slang for either of two items on the mess menu: chicken cacciatore or chicken á la king, both of which feature birds variously deconstructed.

Eleven bang-bang

An army infantryman. Every job in the U.S. military is identified by an MOS (Military Occupation Specialty) code number. An infantryman is MOS 11B ("eleven-bravo"), *b* is the first letter of *bang*, and *bang-bang* pretty much sums up what someone with this MOS does for a living. Alternatives to **eleven bang-bang** include **eleven boom-boom** and, more gruesomely, **eleven bulletstop**. During the Vietnam War era, **eleven bulletstopper** was also commonly used to designate an infantryman.

Eyewash

A verb meaning to hastily and superficially "beautify" a facility in order to impress a visiting dignitary. To **eyewash** typically means cleaning, slapping on a coat of paint, and doing some quick landscaping. "Captain, **eyewash** the company barracks before the end of the day. General's inspecting tomorrow."

Fart sack

Sleeping bag.

Fashion show

A military hazing ritual in which the victim is compelled to don, in rapid succession, all of his complete uniforms, including dress, field, fatigue, summer, and winter. The uniforms as well as the victim's quarters (or bunk and footlocker) are closely inspected. The rationale for the **fashion show** is to create a stressful situation that tests the mettle of the subject/victim.

Fiddler's Green

In sailing lore, **Fiddler's Green** is a kind of paradise, into which deceased sailors are welcomed. It is a lush and pleasant place of everlasting merrymaking and tireless dancing to fiddle tunes that go on for eternity. The earliest printed mention occurs in an 1832 sailor's tale, which describes **Fiddler's Green** as located "nine miles beyond the dwelling of his Satanic majesty." Today, many U.S. Navy petty officers' clubs are named "**Fiddler's Green**," and the phrase is also used in the U.S. Army and the Marine Corps. The *Cavalry Journal* (April 1923) published "Fiddler's Green and other Cavalry Songs by JHS," which cites a campfire tale told by Captain "Sammy" Pearson in the Medicine Bow Mountains of Wyoming, picturing **Fiddler's Green** as the place dead cavalry troopers go. To this day, cavalrymen speak of the dead as having passed on to **Fiddler's Green**. With far greater irony, the name has been applied to at least one Vietnam-era forward base (Fire Support Base, Military Region III, manned by elements of 2d Squadron, 11th Armored Cavalry) and, much more recently, a USMC firebase in Helmand Province, Afghanistan.

Fighting gear

Eating utensils. The term is universal throughout the military but most often heard in the U.S. Navy.

FIGJAM

This acronym, common in the Australian armed forces and borrowed by Americans serving with the Aussies during the Vietnam War, stands for F*uck, I'm Good—Just Ask Me*. An expression of intense self-confidence at once sardonic, ironic, swaggering, and smart alecky, it is typically American, even if it is quintessentially Australian.

First Estate

Medieval European society recognized three "Estates of the realm." The Third Estate was made up of non-peasant commoners; the Second Estate, the nobility; and the First Estate, the clergy. In some quarters of the U.S. military, members of chaplain service are referred to as the **First Estate**.

Flake out

To lie down and sleep—usually for the purpose of a brief nap. "Let me **flake out** in my **fart sack** for a half hour, then wake me up, corporal."

Float

Used as a noun in the U.S. Navy, **float** is a synonym for any cruise assignment. "Is this your first **float**, **Nugget**?"

Fluff 'N' Buff

It's not your father's army or marines. Through the Vietnam Era, these services were notorious for a spit-and-polish approach to uniforms, from fatigues to Class A dress. One of the reforms in the All-Volunteer Force (AVF) was aimed at making a military career more palatable by reducing the level of **chicken shit** (see page 14), including the apparently ceaseless demands that shoes be spit shined and uniforms neatly pressed. These days, the camouflage and other BDU (Battle Dress Uniforms) most troops wear most of the time are not pressed but merely kept clean (washed) and fluff dried without ironing. Footwear—often desert boots, in any case—is no longer spotlessly shined, but merely buffed into a decent appearance.

Fried calamari

One traditional nickname for a U.S. Navy sailor is **squid** (or **squiddie**). A sailor who has met his demise by accidental electrocution—an occupational hazard when high-voltage electrical equipment is operated in the presence of seawater—is called **fried calamari**.

Fried horsecock

Those who tend bars frequented by sailors generally keep something hard and handy below the bar to settle barroom disputes that get physical. Some use a baseball bat, but the old-timers favor a long, thick, unsliced, shrink-wrapped salami or bologna sausage commonly referred to as a **horsecock**. Since sailors are often intimately familiar with this symbol of bartender authority, the fried baloney sausage frequently served in a navy mess is universally called **fried horsecock**.

Fuck the mission, clean the position

On board ship, an order to stop whatever you're doing—no matter how critically important it may seem—and grab a mop. Start swabbing.

Galloping dandruff

Since World War I, the army term for crab lice.

Gasper

One of the more innovative synonyms for a cigarette. "Hey, buddy. Can I bum a **gasper**?" Like *coffin nail* and *cancer stick*, terms familiar in civilian use, **gasper** celebrates the destructive effects of smoking on one's health—in this case, let's rejoice in emphysema.

General's car, the

A wheelbarrow. "Private, I want you to dig up that manure pile, put it in **the general's car**, and dump it in back of the barracks."

Get a hat

To leave—especially common in the USMC. "I have to **get a hat**" or "The lieutenant **got a hat** about fifteen minutes ago."

Gig line

The navy has a name for everything, including the uninterrupted visual line that should be formed by the shirt seam, belt buckle, and trouser zipper of the uniform. New recruits are often unfamiliar with the term, however, and old hands are fond of sending a newbie on a shipwide hunt for a **gig line**—sometimes adding a bulkhead remover and a lefthanded monkey wrench into the expedition as well.

Gofasters

In the U.S. Army, Navy, and Marine Corps, term for sneakers.

Gouge, the

Informal military synonym for "the scoop," in the sense of the latest news about something. "What's **the gouge** on our next liberty?"

Grab-a-Whore

What the troops call "USAG Graf": the U.S. Army Garrison at Grafenwöhr, Germany, which provides support to the Seventh Army Training Command and performs other NATO missions.

Grape

In the submarine service, an easy assignment or easy task is called a **grape**. The term can also be used as a compliment, in the sense of "You made that look so easy." For example: "Pulling a double watch? **Grape** duty for a man like you." The submarine service application of **grape** is not to be confused with its meaning in naval aviation, where a **grape** is a sailor who fuels aircraft. On a carrier flight deck, these sailors are identified by the purple jerseys they wear—hence **grapes**. Also see **Gourd**, p. 137.

Gronk

Submarines are held together with a lot of nuts on a lot of bolts, and if you're worried about springing a leak when you get several hundred feet below the surface, you're going to want to tighten each nut super tight. The process of such application is called **gronk**, after the sound of the groan emitted by the man with the wrench. Conversely, when trying to loosen a **gronked** nut, the wrench wielder will also invariably emit a **gronk.**

Group tightener

Depending on context, marines use this in any of three senses. Range instructors apply a **group tightener** to the sights of a faltering trainee's rifle (they explain) "to improve marksmanship." In fact, the substance applied, oil or some solvent, has no effect other than a hoped-for psychological one, which may be sufficient to goose the recruit successfully through the range course. Senior marines also delight in sending recruits to fetch "a load of **group tighteners**," which, like a left-handed monkey wrench, do not in fact exist. Finally, after spending a hard day working with recruits, especially on the rifle range, marksman instructors gather at the enlisted men's club for a **group tightener** or two or more: a stiff drink to unwind.

G-Spot

In civilian life, the **G-Spot** is short for the **Gräfenberg Spot**, a bean-shaped area of the vagina that many women report as a zone of intense sexual stimulation and arousal. At U.S. Marine Base Camp Pendleton, California, the **G-Spot** is a building housing most of the divisional staff organizations, such as G-1 (personnel), G-2 (intelligence), G-3 (operations), G-4 (logistics), and so on. This is a major difference between life outside and life inside Camp Pendleton.

Happy Hour

On shore, the local bar's interval of half-price drinks. On board a vessel of the United States Navy, one hour of mandatory ship cleaning each and every day. Sometimes it's better to be on shore.

Hockey pucks

Swedish meatballs, a staple of any U.S. Navy mess. These are also known as **road apples**, **porcupines**, and **trail markers**.

Hollywood shower

An excessively long—and therefore water wasting—shower. This is the exact opposite of a **navy shower**. Whereas a **Hollywood shower** is long, luxurious, and wasteful of precious water, a **navy shower** is so brief and unpleasant that it is damn near dry.

How they hangin'?

Used in civilian life, this expression became very common in the U.S. military, beginning in World War II. In both the civilian and military spheres, the question is a friendly inquiry as to one's well-being. Its origin may have been in a military in which much attention was paid to the state of a soldier's genitals (see **short-arms inspection**). Understand that the "they" refers to the testicles, and be aware of the medical fact that, normally, the left testicle descends lower than the right. Perhaps this bears some relation to the folk belief that blood supplied to the right testicle comes from the heart, whereas that to the left arrives via the kidneys. Some evolutionists believe that the asymmetry is an adaptation that helps to prevent injury and constriction.

Ice cream suit

Any all-white uniform, including the U.S. Navy "service dress" (Class A) summer uniform, worn with white shoes, but also the mess dress uniform of all service branches, the military equivalent of white formal evening dress.

Irish pennant

A loose thread on the uniform of a marine or a sailor. This is not a slur on the Irish people, but an allusion to the green color of the Class A uniform—the hue associated with Ireland and the Irish.

Jack-o'-the-Dust

In the modern navy, this is a term sometimes applied to the ship's cook tasked with inventorying ship's stores. It is derived from the night baker on ships of the old navy, who could be seen fleetingly at daybreak, trundling off to his bunk, coated in flour dust, after baking biscuits all night.

JARTGO

Service acronym casually applied to anything, anyone, or any assignment deemed burdensome, tedious, painful, or unpleasant. It stands for *Just Another Reason To Get Out.* A disgruntled sailor grumbles to his shipmate: "Thirty days sitting in Norfolk is **JARTGO**, as far as I'm concerned."

Joe

Coffee, as in "cup of **Joe**." Some etymologists believe that **Joe** as a slang term for coffee is a short form of another colloquial term, *java* or, perhaps, *jamoke*. Others believe it is a reference to Martinson Coffee (formerly called Martinson's Coffee), which is still made but was more popular, especially in the Northeast, some years ago. The owner of the company was one Joseph—Joe—Martinson. Hence, cup of **Joe**. Yet others have suggested that the Joe in "cup of **Joe**" refers to the 1860 song by Stephen Foster, "Old Black Joe," the suggestion being that *black* linked to *Joe* suggests a cup of *black coffee*. The few etymologists with any experience of the U.S. Navy offer another origin for the word: the decree (General Order 99) of straitlaced Secretary of the Navy Josephus Daniels on June 1, 1914, that abolished the "officer's wine mess" aboard ship, thereby making the U.S. Navy officially alcohol free. With the promulgation of that decree, coffee became the strongest drink on naval vessels. It was a cup of **Joe**, short for *Josephus*.

John Wayne

This might refer to any **gung-ho** marine (John Wayne having starred in *The Sands of Iwo Jima*, a quintessential Hollywood treatment of the USMC from 1949) or to the tool that was included in C-Ration cases and used to open the cans. Some of those cans held **John Wayne Crackers**, which were baked round to fit the C-Ration can perfectly.

Last Man Club

Any veterans' organization consisting of former members of military specialties that no longer exist. A group of veteran glider pilots, for instance, would be a Last Man Club. The phrase is also often applied to organizations of veterans of specific campaigns, battles, or engagements (the Bataan Bastards, for example).

Let the dead bury the dead

Leave it alone, and it will take care of itself—an expression of supreme indifference.

Lifer

A term service members apply equally to career military personnel and to those convicted of capital crimes. Because everything in the military is, or sooner or later becomes, an acronym, LIFER is sometimes said to stand for *L*azy *I*ncompetent *F*uck *E*xpecting *R*etirement or, with a somewhat higher degree of literacy, *L*owly *I*ndignant *F*uck *E*vading *R*eality. Many regard the appellation of **lifer** to be a grave insult: "You can call me a moron, a child molester, or even a politician, but never *ever* call me a **lifer dog**." A lifer is instantly recognizable by the large number of **lifer stripes** on the sleeve of his or her Class A uniform, each stripe signifying four years of service. Lifers are universally addicted to **lifer juice**, a.k.a. coffee, not merely for stimulation but because GI java (according to credible sources) kills brain cells, disabling the habitual drinker from making any intelligent decisions, such as the decision to leave the military. Indeed, soldiers, airmen, marines, and sailors designate any coffee cup that is deeply stained, indicating years of use unwashed, a **lifer cup**. On board any U.S. Navy vessel, the biggest collection of **lifer cups** is found in the **Lifer Locker**, the lounge reserved for petty officers first class

(E-6). Because the term **lifer** is inherently derogatory, suggesting a prison sentence rather than a patriotic career, commanders occasionally issue an order forbidding the use of the term, even in jest. When this happens, **refil** is often used. This is not so much a misspelling of *refill* as it is a scrambled version of **lifer**, with whatever derogatory connotation *refill* implies.

Lima Mike November

The NATO phonetic version of the acronym LMN, which is an emphatic form of demurral in response to a request for some action or favor: *Lick My Nuts.*

Mating mosquitoes

The highly imaginative alternative to what is officially called in the U.S. Army "a corporal." The sleeve emblem is two somewhat concave chevrons, one atop the other, which suggested to some sex-starved soldier (as who among soldiers is not?) the winged coupling of a pair of *Culisetae longiareolatae*. See also **mosquito wing**.

Meat identifier

Military food is to food what military music is to music. This being the case, military cooks often include characteristic side dishes to identify the otherwise indistinguishable meat that makes up the main dish. The presence of mashed potatoes and gravy indicates turkey; horseradish implies prime rib; applesauce, pork chops. Sailors, soldiers, airmen, and marines call such side dishes **meat identifiers**.

Military tan

The distinctive suntan a modern soldier or marine acquires. Clad in a BDU (battle-dress uniform) that covers everything except—and only sometimes—face, neck, throat, and part of the forearm, the service member exhibits a healthy glow on the face and extremities that is set off by the pasty pallor that characterizes the rest of his physiognomy.

Mosquito wing

The single concave chevron of a U.S. Army private, first class. See **Mating mosquitoes**.

MRE

The MRE (*M*eal, *R*eady-to-*E*at), a 3,600-calorie combat ration attractively packaged in a dung brown plastic pouch, replaced the earlier C- and E-rations. Precooked beef stew, sliced ham, chicken, and Swiss steak are typical MRE varieties, although everyone who has tried them agrees that they all have in common the quality of inedibility. Particularly despised (in the U.S. Army and Marine Corps) are MRE beef franks, originally known as **beans and motherfuckers** or the **5 fingers of death**. Later, when the portion was reduced to four franks and stripped of beans and sauce, the meal was rechristened **4 dicks of death**. Another popular alternative name is **bag nasty**. Like many other proverbially unpleasant things, the MRE has inspired GI verse:

Once there was an MRE,
Purpose being plain to see,
Meals Ready to Eat,
Keeps men on their feet,
Or squatting in misery.

And, like all military acronyms, **MRE** has spawned multiple interpretations, including *M*eals *R*arely *E*aten, *M*eals *R*ejected *by* *E*thiopians, and (on a more ecumenical note) *M*eals *R*ejected *by* *E*veryone. The Canadian armed forces call their version of the **MRE** the IMP, said to stand for I *M*ust *P*uke.

Mustang

In the U.S. Army, Navy, and Marines, a **mustang** is an officer who was promoted from the enlisted ranks— much as a fine, spirited riding horse can be broken from a mustang in the wild.

No excuse

The proper military response when one admits fault or unconditional responsibility for some error or failure. *Captain:* "Can you explain why the ammo locker was left unsecured, Seaman?" *Seaman:* "**No excuse, Sir!**"

Nugget

A U.S. Navy sailor on his initial cruise.

Number one, number ten, number ten thousand

A scale of misery improvised by GIs during the Vietnam War: number one is the best, number ten is the worst, and number ten thousand is the way things usually are.

Nut to butt

In the army, an instruction to form a compact single-file line, as in the mess hall.

Officer's candy

What sailors call the deodorant cake placed in a urinal.

Old Soldier's Home

The latrine.

Pillows of death

Sailor's term for mess compartment ravioli.

Real World, the

What National Guardsmen and Army Reservists call civilian life when they are summoned away from it to active duty.

Records Manglement

Records Management.

Red Weenie

Disparaging term for the Good Conduct Medal, which is awarded to enlisted and NCO personnel in all U.S. service branches, except the U.S. Air Force, for satisfactory service—or, basically, for not having been caught doing anything particularly wrong. "Weenie" implies insignificant, which is what this decoration, awarded once every three years, pretty much is. The USAF discontinued the decoration in 2006 on the grounds that "normal" behavior should not be singled out for special recognition.

Ricky

Short for "recruit"—a sailor still in boot camp. A **ricky** uses a **ricky sweep** (his bare hands) to clean the deck, a **ricky iron** (his right hand) to press his uniform, and a **ricky girlfriend** (that same right hand) to engage in **ricky boxing** (masturbating). Since all of this takes a lot out of a **ricky**, he consumes plenty of **ricky rockets** (homemade energy drinks compounded of soda, coffee, sugar, sports drinks, and artificial sweeteners) to keep his eyes open.

Roast beast

Technically, roast beef served in any military mess hall. But since it is often impossible to determine whether the foodstuff is beef or something else, the term **roast beast** is applied to any nonvegetable cooked food that is vaguely brown and vaguely meat-like.

Salad bar

The array of service ribbons worn on a military uniform.

Seaman Schmuckatelli

Generic name for the "typical" U.S. Navy enlisted sailor. Like "G. I. Joe" in World War II. Not to be confused with **Seaman Timmy**, the equivalent of "John Doe," used to refer to a sailor, actual identity unknown, who **popped the puppy** (see **screw the pooch**), causing some major foul-up.

Shield of Shame

Nickname for the insignia of the Adjutant General's Corps, which has no combat role and whose members, therefore, always remain safe and secure "in the rear with the gear."

Shit

Generally, the most useful word, or word root, in the United States military. To wit:

S.H.I.T.

*S*outh *H*udson *I*nstitute of *T*echnology, a.k.a. U.S. Military Academy, located overlooking the Hudson River at West Point, New York.

Shit detail

A difficult, thankless, futile assignment.

Shithook

The human hand; the origin is the hygienic function of the left hand in the absence of toilet paper.

Shit on a Shingle

See **SOS**.

SOL

*S*hit *O*utta *L*uck. Basically, to be screwed.

Shit paper

Slang for toilet paper in general and for the few squares of TP that are thoughtfully packed with **MREs**.

Shit rolls downhill, the

An immutable law of military physics, which dictates that the lowest-ranking available individual is always and invariably the one who receives blame and/or the worst assignment (i.e., the **shit detail**). Under no circumstances does shit ever roll uphill, say, from a second lieutenant to a colonel.

Three S's, the

Shit, shower, and *shave*: the program of a soldier's morning ablutions. On inspection days, add a fourth, *shine*, referring to shoes and brass.

I shit you not

An emphatic assertion of earnestness. "Fail in this assignment and you're busted down to private. **I shit you not**."

Shit can

Noun, synonym for *wastebasket*. Verb, throw in the trash, cease and desist some course of action, reject or abandon an idea, notion, desire, or aspiration. "Private Pyle, the sooner you **shit can** your delusions of someday, somehow making corporal, the less disappointed you will be in yourself."

Short arm

Penis—almost always used in the context of **short arm inspection**.

Short arm inspection

Cursory examination of the male genitals usually carried out by enlisted medical personnel in an effort to detect the early signs of sexually transmitted disease.

Show a Leg

A naval expression born of ancient tradition, "**Show a leg**" is an imperative meaning *Wake up!* It is used to rouse a sleeping sailor when it is his or her turn to take the watch. The expression comes from a time when sailors were unofficially but universally permitted to sleep with their girlfriends or prostitutes aboard ship when the ship was in port. The ladies quickly learned to keep their stockings on in bunk or hammock ("show a leg") to distinguish themselves from the men, thereby avoiding a rude awakening kick or jab.

Slick sleeve

The U.S. Navy likes to put stripes and insignias on the sleeves of the uniforms its personnel wear. A sailor at the E-1 rating, entry-level and unrated, starts out with a **slick sleeve**: no stripes, no insignia, no nothing.

Smurf suit

The solid blue sweatshirt and sweatpants issued to a sailor recruit on arrival at boot camp. Several days will pass before he or she is issued a uniform, and, in the meantime, the bright blue PT (physical training) ensemble brings to mind the cartoon blue skin of a Smurf.

Snot locker

For U.S. Navy and Marine Corps personnel, a synonym for the human nose. It is a play on the phrase *shot locker*, the strongly framed compartment on ships of the wooden navy where cannon shot was stored.

Soldier's breakfast, a

Cigarette and a cup of coffee.

SOS

Shit On a Shingle; also, *Same Old Shit*. In 1908, *SOS* was adopted as the international radiotelegraph Morse Code signal for distress. At some time during World War II, those same initials were adopted in the enlisted men's mess as a signal of specifically gustatory distress. A staple of World War II military cuisine was creamed chipped beef on toast, unofficially and universally dubbed *Shit On a Shingle*: **SOS**. The utility of this acronym rapidly increased as the expression came to be more widely applied to signify any old lies, chores, or routines the army dished up day after day: *Same Old Shit*. In this latter sense, **SOS** entered, and has lingered in, general civilian speech, although it is sometimes sanitized to mean *Same Old Stuff* or simply abridged and reduplicated to **same old same old**. When **SOS** went civilian, the enlisted crowd started looking for a new name for creamed chipped beef on toast (still, as in World War II, a venerated standby of military cuisine) and seems to have settled on the charming **creamed foreskin**, a term that arguably makes for a better metaphor, since *shit* on a shingle suggests *ground* beef rather than *chipped* beef.

Soup cooler

Yet another military synonym for the human mouth.

Spankers and clankers

U.S. Navy dress uniform, which includes a sword (spanker) and pendant medals (clankers)—not the service ribbons worn on a Class A uniform.

Steel Beach

Off-duty relaxation on board a ship—offering all the benefits of a real beach without the beach.

Steel Beach picnic

Any shipboard celebration out on the weather decks (exposed decks, as opposed to interior, "below decks" space) is called a **Steel Beach picnic**. Barbecue is generally in abundance.

Stone soup

A bad situation offering few options, but one that a soldier is determined to endure and make the best of. The source of the expression is the hobo "meal" made of hot water and a stone "added for flavor."

Striker

Traditional term for a sailor undergoing on-the-job training (OJT) for a designated specialty or technical rating. For example, an aspiring signalman is a "signalman striker."

Suds Row

On-post housing section allocated to married NCOs, so called because sergeants' wives traditionally did officers' laundry to supplement their husband's meager income. That practice has long since vanished, but the name has stuck.

Swab

In the United States Navy, this word has the distinction of referring both to any sailor and to any mop, behind which any sailor often finds himself or herself.

The Mother-in-Law of the Army

Fort Leavenworth, Kansas. The name comes from the historical fact that soldiers' families often remained in and around Fort Leavenworth when their husbands were posted either farther west (during the days of the Indian Wars) or overseas. Others insist that the name derives from the multitude of Army daughters on base, who selectively married young officers who had promising prospects of promotion.

Things on springs

Name for the array of uniforms, fittings, and equipment laid out for inspection—according to a strictly prescribed order—on a marine's bunk. Also called **junk on the bunk**.

Tube steak

This synonym for a hot dog is not confined to the U.S. military but is widely used in all service branches—except by soldiers, sailors, marines, and airmen who prefer the more vivid "**dangling sirloin**."

Vampire liberty

Liberty, for sailors, is time off in port. **Vampire liberty** is a day off given to a sailor as a reward for donating a pint of blood in a blood drive.

Voluntold

A totally voluntary assignment that is absolutely mandatory. "Gentlemen, your attendance at the scheduled four-hour hygiene lecture is entirely **voluntold**."

Whiskey Tango Foxtrot

NATO phonetic alphabet signifying WTF—W*hat* T*he* F*uck*. In most situations, the expression conveys the soldier's/sailor's/marine's/airman's state of mind perfectly and comprehensively.

YGFBKM

Personnel of the American armed forces never met an acronym they didn't like, and while many are obscure as to meaning, almost all are at least easy to turn into a pronounceable syllable or two. **YGFBKM** apparently got out of hand, however. It stands for *You've Gotta Fucking Be Kidding Me*, a standard expression of routine exasperation.

You Bet Your Life

During the Vietnam War era, this was the informal name for the final test exercise required for graduation from various especially arduous military training courses, such as the Air Force survival course. The name comes from the long-running quiz show hosted by Groucho Marx on radio and television from 1947 to 1961: "You Bet Your Life."

Young Lions

Young soldiers and marines who are fierce, hungry for glory, burning with zeal, and utterly untested. The phrase is applied by veterans of combat both sincerely and with wary irony.

Zero-three

A Marine Corps haircut: zero inches on the sidewalls, three inches on top. Also known as **high and tight**.

TWO

Cake Eaters and Chicken Guts

*Military Courtesy and
Command Authority*

★ ★

Above my paygrade

The standard response to a question you don't want to answer. At face value, the phrase means that the issue raised is so important that it can be addressed only by someone higher in rank and grade than oneself. The savvy inquirer understands, however, that, as is true of most military language, the face value of the phrase is not its real meaning, to wit: "Go away. I don't want to get involved."

> **Q:** "Should I tell the colonel that he has made a mistake?"
>
> **A:** "Well, that's **above my paygrade**, Joe."

Admiral and *Admiral's March*

Officially, an admiral is a flag officer of the highest rank in the U.S. naval services (U.S. Navy and Coast Guard), but the word is often used as dismissive slang for *sailor*, as in "Hey, **Admiral**, swab the damn deck." All petty officers would point out that calling an ordinary seaman an admiral is an insult to both seamen *and* admirals. Members of the ship's band know that when an admiral climbs aboard for an official visit they are expected to strike up the **Admiral's March**, a lively tune in quick cut time that encourages everyone, the admiral included, to step lively. No sailor can hear the march without running the unofficial lyrics through his or her head: "He's a bum, he's a bum, he's a rotten lousy bum ..."

Admiral of the Narrow Seas

A sailor who, seasick, drunk, or both, has just upchucked into the lap of the sailor sitting next to him. The phrase is current and believed to have originated as early as the eighteenth century—the era of wooden ships and iron men, many of whom apparently suffered from dyspepsia.

Alpha Mike Foxtrot

The NATO phonetic expression of the initials *AMF*, this is used as shorthand for "A*dios,* M*other* F*ucker*," a salutation that may be used as a friendly farewell to barracks companions or as a valediction addressed to an enemy on whom you are about to pull the trigger. Context is everything.

Alpha Unit

The spouse of a United States Marine.

Aluminum U.

The United States Air Force Academy. The nickname was born in an era when most advanced, high-performance aircraft were made of this metal. These days, "Carbon Fiber Reinforced U." would be more accurate, if pedantic.

Anchor clanker

What U.S. Naval personnel call a boatswain's mate, and what U.S. Marine Corps personnel call *anyone* of *any* rank in the U.S. Navy.

BAM

This acronym came into use among marines during World War II to refer to a Woman Marine. Reportedly, it stood for *broad-assed Marine,* but the women were told it "officially" stood for B*eautiful* A*merican* M*arine.* During the Vietnam War era, a male marine who was assigned to noncombat administrative duties—which were the

usual province of Women Marines—was referred to as a
ball-bearing BAM. The **BAM** acronym is extinct in the
modern USMC.

Band-Aid

A Vietnam War-era medic.

Beaters 'n' bleaters

Military marching band members. While it is true that
the U.S. armed forces employs many superb professional
musicians, marching band fare remains the perennial
index against which many other unpleasant aspects of
military life are measured. These personnel are also called
tooters. Consider: "Military justice is to justice what
military music is to music," or "Army food is to food
what army music is to music," and so on.

Bird, Ball, and Chain

Disgruntled grunt's term for the U.S. Marine Corps
emblem, which features an eagle, a globe, and an anchor
(with a rope rather than a chain).

BLOB

Used in aircraft operations, this is an acronym for B*ig* L*ump* O*n* B*oard* and denotes any nonfunctional passenger. Alternative designations include **deadhead** (a term applied in the civilian transportation industry to any nonpaying passenger), **sandbag** (inert weight; ballast), and **strap-hanger**. Less expressively, **POB** is also sometimes used, signifying P*ersonnel* O*n* B*oard*.

Cadidiot

What noncommissioned U.S. Army soldiers call an officer *cadet*.

Cake Eater

Among the civilian population, this is a working-class synonym for a wealthy person. In the U.S. Navy, it is a sailor who reenlists. The civilian meaning is derived from "Let them eat cake," the infamous quotation, universally but mistakenly attributed to Queen Marie Antoinette, regarding the French poor, who were starving because they had no bread. The navy meaning derives from the custom of presenting a sailor with a cake upon reenlistment.

Captain of the Head

The marine grunt or navy sailor responsible for cleaning bathrooms and toilets. Both on board ship and in the marine or navy barracks, the washroom is called the *head*, since, on old-school sailing vessels, toilet facilities were located belowdecks in the forepart ("head") of the ship.

Chair Force

What soldiers, sailors, and marines call the United States Air Force.

Charm School

Generic term used by enlisted personnel to identify any professional course offered exclusively to officers.

Chest candy

Medals and battle ribbons. The connotation of the phrase depends entirely on context and is conveyed by tone. **Chest candy** may be an expression of awe and admiration—"They don't give out that kind of **chest candy** for nothing"—or contempt: "A lot of **chest candy** stuck to that empty suit."

Chicken guts

Also known as **loafer's loops**, this is the common name for the aiguillette, the decoratively braided, looped cord worn as an emblem of office by military officers assigned to such special staff duties as aide to senior government officials or aide to military officers of flag rank. Presidential aides wear gold chicken guts on their right shoulder, whereas aides to other officials and to flag officers wear braided loafer's loops on their left shoulder: red and gold braids for the army and marines, blue and gold for the navy. The number of loops in the aiguillette equals the number of stars signifying the rank of the officer to whom the aide is assigned. Aides to the president and to (four-star) generals or admirals wear four loops. The aide to a major general (two-star) gets a two-loop set of chicken guts. And so on.

Chuck

During the Vietnam War era, what black marines called white marines (at least among themselves). The word is a variation on "Mister Charlie," a longtime African American term for "the white man." According to an article by John Cowley in *The Journal of Folklore Research* (28, nos. 2/3), "Shack Bullies and Levee Contractors: Bluesmen as Ethnographers," the origin of *Mister Charlie* dates to several blues songs, which are loosely based on one Charley Lowrence, a Mississippi contractor who paid black laborers notoriously low wages to build and repair levees in the 1920s. Neither **Chuck** nor "Mister Charlie" should be confused with "Charlie" as the familiar term among white and black soldiers for the Viet Cong. This sense of "Charlie" was a truncation of **Victor Charlie**, the military phonetic alphabet representation of "VC"— V*iet* C*ong.*

Clerks and jerks

Collective name for administrative, support, and other strictly noncombat personnel, also known as **chairborne commandos**.

COB

Submariner's acronym for *Chief Of the Boat* (the senior chief petty officer on board), it is always pronounced as it's spelled and replaces the chief's given name. "**COB**, make your depth 300 feet."

Cookie pushers

What military personnel call U.S. State Department officials who make unnecessary, ineffectual, temporizing, or lily-livered moves when decisive actions are called for.

Cousin

A soldier, airman, marine, or sailor from the military of an allied nation. For instance, a United States Marine might refer to a British Royal Marine as **cousin** or to a UK unit fighting alongside his own outfit as "our **cousins**."

Crumb Catcher

Military jargon for the human mouth, as in "Shut your damn **crumb catcher** before I shut it for you, **Maggot**."

CSMO

Officially, the acronym meaning "Close Station, March Order," meaning "end of mission" (close the station and march out). Unofficially, **CSMO** is a command to *Collect [your] Shit [and] Move Out.* "I've been assigned this cubicle, private. **CSMO** on the double."

Dick

You don't have to be in the U.S. armed forces to use this familiar term, but it is rarely heard outside of the American military when in combination with the following: **dick cheese**, a useless member of a team or unit; **dick holster**, the human mouth—also reported as a reference to a female marine; and **dick skinners**, hands.

DILLIGAF

Naval acronym one uses to spare the effort of actually saying, "Do I look like I give a fuck?" If you are especially emphatic in your indifference, you hold the final *f* sound to indicate **DILLIGAFF**, signifying, "Do I look like I give a flying fuck?" This is the proper response to a shipmate who brings you personal news *he* considers very exciting or critically important.

Dinner plate for marines

By long tradition, the dress blues worn by enlisted U.S. Navy sailors include bell-bottom trousers that have, in place of a fly, a large front flap that is closed by thirteen buttons, officially signifying the thirteen original states of the Union, but informally referred to as "thirteen chances to change your mind." It is unclear whether those who refer to this unique feature of military regalia as a **dinner plate for marines** intend disrespect to the marines, the navy, both, or, in fact, neither.

Dog robber

A general officer's aide. His or her duties are so varied and generally so obscure that no one knows how to describe them. This phrase is the best guess.

Fart sack

Sleeping bag. Never to be confused with a **fart cart**, a ground-based air pressure unit sometimes used to start jet engines, or (for that matter) with **farts and darts**, the airman's term for the decorations on the dress-uniform cap visor of a USAF field grade officer (major or above).

A more official, but not necessarily more accurate, description of the decoration would be four silver clouds from which lightning bolts (two per cloud) and arrows (one per cloud) project.

Field grade weather

U.S. Air Force field grade officers (major and above) spend a lot of time flying a desk, but they do like to get into the cockpit once in a while, provided the weather is exceptionally fine—**field grade weather**. Low ceilings, low visibility, precipitation, and cross winds—those they leave to company grade officers (captain and below).

Floating bellhop

This is what members of the U.S. Army call any member of the U.S. Navy. Interestingly, soldiers as well as sailors call any member of the U.S. Marine Corps, more simply, a **bellhop.** Both terms date from the days when hotel bellmen wore more elaborate uniforms than they do now.

Fobbit

A term that came into being among the regular U.S. uniformed military forces during the wars in Iraq and Afghanistan, which developed in the wake of the terrorist attacks against the United States on September 11, 2001, **Fobbit** combines the acronym *FOB,* standing for *Forward Operations Base,* with *Hobbit,* a member of the diminutive Middle-Earth race that populates J. R. R. Tolkien's fiction, principally *The Hobbit* and *The Lord of the Rings.* The term is disparagingly applied to noncombat support personnel—mostly contract civilians, but also military—who never poke their heads outside of the FOB, where they might get shot at or blown up. The FOB is sometimes referred to as **Fobbitville.** Also see **Tocroach.**

Former Marine

Nonexistent. A marine is always a marine, even after retirement from the Corps, never applies this phrase to himself or herself, and objects (strenuously) when anyone else attempts to apply it to him or her.

Fortitudine

In 1883, *Semper Fidelis*—"Always faithful"—was officially adopted as the motto of the United States Marine Corps. Prior to this, the best-known USMC motto was the Latin **Fortitudine**, meaning "With fortitude" or "With courage." It was in use as early as before the War of 1812, along with another Latin motto, *Per Mare, Per Terram* (By Sea, By Land), which the USMC shared with the British Royal Marines. A third motto, "To the Shores of Tripoli," referring to the 1805 Battle of Derne against the Barbary Pirates in Tripoli during the First Barbary War of 1801-1805, went out of use in 1843, but is remembered in the opening lines of *The Marines' Hymn*:

> From the Halls of Montezuma,
> To the shores of Tripoli

The marines, by the way, hardly have a monopoly on the current motto, *Semper Fidelis,* which has been used by numerous notable families since as early as 1180, and by such cities as Abbeville and St. Malo (France), Calvi (Corsica), Exeter (England), Lviv (Ukraine), and even

White Plains, New York. Various military formations throughout the world use it, including the 11th Infantry Regiment of the U.S. Army, and the marine corps of Portugal and the Republic of China (Taiwan), as well as the Swiss Grenadiers, the Hungarian Government Guard, the Romanian secret service, and the Submarine Force of the Chilean Navy, among others.

Fruit fly

A war correspondent or reporter. The precise etymology of the name is uncertain, although it is certainly derogatory. Fruit flies are annoying and they multiply rapidly. They are attracted to rot (whether a dirty, embarrassing story or the casualties of combat). The term may also be related to **gadfly**, derived from the fly that annoys horses and other animals and that is used to denote any professional troublemaker or troublemaking critic, and the idea of "fruit" suggests a derogatory reference to a homosexual or "sissy."

FUNGUS

F*uck* Y*ou*, N*ew* G*uy*, U S*uck*: Constructive encouragement given to a recruit or, in the U.S. Navy, a newbie shipmate.

Gadget

Any enlisted man or woman who is temporarily promoted to a position of increased responsibility to fill an urgent need. There is no corresponding increase in pay.

George

The name applied to the most junior officer on board a U.S. Navy ship, this is actually a corruption of an unofficial acronym, **JORG**, which stands for J*unior* O*fficer* R*equiring* G*uidance.* Some insist on putting an *E* on the end: **JORGE**—J*unior* O*fficer* R*equiring* G*eneral* E*ducation.*

God Junior-Grade

This term for any superior officer with an inflated sense of his or her authority or ability is derived from the U.S. Navy's lieutenant junior-grade (LTJG, O-2) rank, the equivalent of an army, air force, or marine first lieutenant.

Good Humor Man

In the opinion of just about everyone—USAF, USA, USMC, and the USN itself—this is what the short-sleeve summer whites make every navy noncom and officer look like. Only thing is, nowadays, where do you find an *actual* Good Humor Man?

Ground pounder

Synonym for **grunt**, a marine infantryman.

Hairy eyeball

Uncomfortably close scrutiny. "You'd better not foul this up. The captain's been giving you the **hairy eyeball** lately."

Hershey bar

What soldiers call the small rectangular stripe worn on the lower right sleeve of a Class A (dress) uniform, denoting six months of overseas service. A bar is added for each six months, so that those who serve abroad long enough look like they are wearing a stack of little candy bars on their sleeve.

Hinge

There is a widespread belief in the U.S. Navy that promotion to the rank of lieutenant commander requires a lobotomy, which naval personnel mistakenly equate with removal of precisely half of the officer's brain. At the time of the removal of this portion of brain, a hinge is installed in the skull to permit reinsertion of the part when and if the O-4 is promoted to O-5, commander. A side effect of installing the hinge is the limitation of head movement to up and down only, which allows the lieutenant commander to nod in perpetual agreement with his commanding officer. So critical is the hinge to the O-4 rank that sailors feel entitled to call any lieutenant commander a **hinge**, though never in his or her presence.

Hollow Bunny

Post-Vietnam era term for an incompetent female officer. Presumably derived from a sexist equation of women with Playboy Bunnies crossed, perhaps, with the image of a hollow Easter chocolate bunny, the phrase is precisely the equivalent of **empty suit** applied to an incompetent, useless male officer.

Hot Dog

In the U.S. Air Force, a young, arrogant, showy, aggressive, and usually dangerous fighter pilot. In the U.S. Navy, a sexually active sailor.

House mouse

Enlisted man pressed into service by a company officer or a drill instructor to run errands and assist in demonstrations. Although "promotion" to **house mouse** is strictly unofficial, it often serves as a prelude to an actual promotion.

Hug squad

The extremely unofficial name for the team of soldiers who notify next of kin of a service member killed in the line of duty. The "squad" usually consists of a Casualty Assistance Officer (CAO) and a chaplain (i.e., a **sky pilot**).

I Believe Button

Like a "Panic Button," the **I Believe Button** is a mythical piece of hardware that substitutes for rationality when there is no time to develop actual understanding. The modern U.S. Navy is a highly technical environment, and when an NCO or officer spews complex technical details at an uncomprehending seaman, it is sometimes necessary simply to tell him to do what he's told and not to worry about such details as, say, *consequences*: "Seaman Doe, just press the goddam **I Believe Button** and we'll analyze it later."

ID10T

Something you send a fresh seaman recruit to fetch: "Johnson, fill out a Form **ID10T** right away and bring it back to me. On the double—or it's your ass." The military phonetic pronunciation is *Eye Dee Ten Tango,* but, write it down, and what it spells looks like *IDIOT.* Recruits are asked to fetch a variety of mythical items, ranging from the classic **left-handed monkey wrench** to the more innovative **bulkhead remover**.

JO

"Joe": any *Junior Officer.* **JOJO**—"Joe-Joe": any junior officer you can't stand the sight or sound of.

Knuckle dragger

In the U.S. Army, a motor pool mechanic. In the U.S. Navy, an engineer or mechanic on any nuclear-powered vessel (aircraft carrier or submarine) or a boatswain's mate on any other craft.

Leaning Shithouse

During the Vietnam War, soldiers belonging to the logistics command, known as 1st FASCOM, wore shoulder patches with a thick pointer theoretically indicating eleven o'clock. To the reasonably imaginative, however, it looked like an old-fashioned outhouse leaning precariously to the left.

Little Prick

Any graduate of the U.S. Army's Leadership Preparation Course—LPC—who throws his weight around, barks orders, and gives others a hard time risks designation as a **Little Prick**—L*ittle*P*ri*C*k.*

Living the dream

Among U.S. service personnel, this is the stock reply to the question, "How you doin' today?" If the question is from a superior officer, the reply is rendered with full military courtesy: "**Living the dream**, Sir!" Translation: "My job sucks, you suck, and I'm totally miserable . . . sir." The concept conveyed by this phrase sometimes takes the form of an acronym, **LTDB,** L*iving* T*he* D*ream,* B*aby*, which, however, would never be used by way of reply to a superior officer.

Maggot

In nature, the larval stage of the common fly and other insects. In the USMC, a brand-new recruit—i.e., the very lowest form of life imaginable. Half-hearted marines, who do everything they can to get themselves discharged, are also referred to as **maggots**, no matter how many years they have in the Corps.

Make it so

Instead of saying "Do it," a U.S. Navy skipper may punctuate a command with the imperative **Make it so.** This is derived from the captain's traditional response to the officer of the deck's (OOD) routine announcement of the arrival of twelve noon. At this, the skipper replies, "Make it so," with the unmistakable implication that, aboard ship, it *cannot* be noon until the captain says it *is* noon. Such is absolute authority in the United States military.

MARINE

To a sailor, this is an acronym for *Muscles Are Required, Intelligence Not Essential* (or *Not Expected*) or *Marines Always Ride In Navy Equipment.*

Marvin the ARVN

What U.S. soldiers dismissively called troops of the Army of the Republic of Vietnam (ARVN—the South Vietnamese army).

MidShitHead

The affectionate title sailors substitute for *midshipman,* a Naval Academy or Naval ROTC student who takes a summer cruise on *your* vessel to get "real navy" experience before returning to classes.

Naviguesser

A less-than-flattering alternative to the *navigator* who is part of a U.S. Air Force or U.S. Navy aircrew.

New meat

A combat replacement, drawn from the pool of raw recruits. Any "piece" of **new meat** generally finds himself on the receiving end of two kinds of special treatment by the combat veterans. First, he is shunned, since the belief is that he will screw up and get himself killed, almost certainly taking with him anyone unfortunate enough to be nearby. Second, he is subjected to the **New Man Rule**, which means that he is immediately assigned to the point position—that is, to the front of the squad, platoon, or company advancing in combat. Rationale: "Taking the point" generously provides him with accelerated combat experience. Real reason: He will draw enemy fire, thereby preserving the more useful combat veterans by taking them out of the crosshairs. **New meat** synonyms include **boot**, **cherry**, **green troop**, **newbie**, **newfer**, and, more directly, **fucking new guy**.

NFO

Stands for N*aval* F*light* O*fficer,* a person the USAF refers to as a Weapons Officer. The NFO flies in tandem with or alongside the pilot—the position depending on the design of the aircraft—and operates the weapons on the aircraft. This is a vital function, but, much of the time, the NFO has little or nothing to do and so is called, quite unflatteringly, a **talking kneeboard**—named after the long narrow board sometimes secured to a pilot's knee on which is affixed notes and orders or a blank pad on which he can make notes (see **Plastic brains**).

Nob Hill

On military bases, the housing area reserved for high-ranking married officers is often informally referred to as **Nob Hill**, which is the name of the San Francisco neighborhood traditionally associated with the wealthy and aristocratic. Presumably, the "Nob" in the original Nob Hill was a shortened form of *noble, nobility, nobleman,* and perhaps *nabob.* In nineteenth-century San Francisco, the area was often called "Snob Hill."

Noted

Reply given by a naval officer to an officer of inferior rank or an enlisted sailor who requests anything resembling a favor. For example:

> *Sailor*: "Sir, if I can have that requisition from you now, I can file it early and begin my liberty."
> *Officer*: **Noted.**

Officer Material

The purest distillation of GI irony. When a soldier calls a comrade-in-arms "officer material," he or she invariably means just the opposite, identifying the trooper in question as a screw-up first class.

Pecker checker

The enlisted medic (army and air force) or corpsman (navy and marines) assigned to dispensary duty. Traditionally, a big part of this person's job is identifying and even treating sexually transmitted diseases (STDs). Alternative titles of honor include **chancre mechanic**, **clap checker**, **pricksmith**, and **penis machinist**.

Petticoat command

Originally, a **petticoat command** was any order issued by a commanding officer that was believed to have been influenced or dictated by his wife (a wearer of petticoats). An order declaring certain saloons off-limits might be interpreted by disgruntled grunts as a **petticoat command**. With repeated use, the phrase came to mean an order that may have been unduly influenced by *any* unqualified, unauthorized adviser, typically a civilian but not necessarily a wife and not necessarily female. Use of the term is often a vote of no-confidence in a commanding officer.

Phone colonel

The step from lieutenant colonel to colonel is bigger than the names of these ranks might imply to a civilian. No one knows this better than a lieutenant colonel, who answers the phone "Colonel Smith" in the hope that the party on the other end of the line will take him for a full colonel. Lieutenant colonels are the Rodney Dangerfields of field-grade officers. They don't get no respect. They're called **light colonel** (Lt. Col.) or even **popcorn colonel** because the oak leaf rank insignia looks like a popcorn kernel. (*Kernel*: *colonel*—get it?)

Pier Queers

What USAF airmen call USN sailors, who, in turn, call airmen, quite simply, **queers**.

POG

A marine's term for a nonmarine, the acronym stands for P*erson* O*ther than a* G*runt,* "grunt" being a term for an enlisted member of the Marine Corps (see **snuffy**).

Puddle Pirate

A member of the United States Coast Guard (according to members of the United States Navy).

Purple Shaft, the (Order of the)

To be given the shaft is, of course, to be punished or otherwise treated unfairly: screwed. To be given the *purple* shaft is to be *royally* screwed, purple being the traditional color of kings and queens. The expression is also a play on *Purple Heart*, the decoration awarded to U.S. military personnel wounded in action; hence, the **Order of the Purple Shaft**. If the shafting in question is particularly egregious, the **Order of the Purple Shaft** may be awarded with "**Barbed Wire Clusters**" or "**Horseshit Clusters**":

> *John*: "Johnson's ass landed in the brig."
> *Jane*: "Got the Purple Shaft?"
> *John*: "With Horseshit Clusters."

Queer

What a U.S. Navy sailor calls a U.S. Air Force airman. Compare **Queer** on p. 206.

Rectal cranial inversion

To have one's head up one's ass—a condition believed to be common among company-grade officers and universal among those of field grade.

REMF

A remarkably official-looking acronym that stands for *Rear Echelon MotherFucker*—in other words, a non-combat desk soldier, sailor, marine, or airman, who shuffles papers and, in the process, somehow makes extra work for you.

Ring knocker

This nickname for a graduate of any of the service academies—West Point, Annapolis, U.S. Air Force Academy—refers to the habit these officers have of "absent-mindedly" tapping their class ring on any convenient surface (often the top of an officer's club or nightclub bar) so as to announce himself or herself as an academy graduate.

ROAD

Acronym signifying R*etired* O*n* A*ctive* D*uty.* In other words, a lazy do-nothing. The term is typically applied to a soldier, sailor, airman, or marine who is marking time within weeks or months of retirement.

Rotorhead

In all the services, a helicopter pilot.

Sand crab

What U.S. Navy sailors call civilian civil service employees or civilian contractors on board ship. A **sand crab** inhabits beaches and survives as a scavenger.

Sarge

A title U.S. Army sergeants gladly welcome, but USMC sergeants most forcefully reject—with raised voice and boot to hindquarters.

Self-loading cargo

Passengers—typically aboard a military transport aircraft.

Senile chief

Affectionate (*not!*) nickname for the senior chief petty officer aboard a ship of the U.S. Navy. The **senile chief** routinely retires to his rack for sixty to ninety minutes of sleep after chowing down in the mess. This is referred to as **SERP:** *Senior Enlisted Rest Period.* Reportedly, **SERP** more than occasionally includes a nonregulation libation.

Shake 'n' Bake

An officer who has been rapidly promoted because of his or her quick progression through the necessary military prep courses and schools, but who has neither combat nor other field experience. Sometimes known by the name of another easily prepared food product, **Reddi-wip**.

Shavetail

What everyone, both above and below him, calls a U.S. Army second lieutenant. Doubtless, the nickname reflects the short Officer Candidate School haircut newly commissioned officers wear, but the origin of the term dates from the days when the army mule was the principal form of cargo and equipment transport in the service. Mule handlers would shave the tails of newly broken animals so that they could be easily distinguished from the better-seasoned mules.

Shoe clerk

USAF term for the holder of a desk job, a military bureaucrat who has no understanding of, say, combat, but who is quite convinced that the pencil he pushes keeps the Air Force flying.

Short seabag, to report on board with a

Said of a sailor perceived to be deficient in basic intellect. A "short seabag" is a term used to refer to a sailor lacking any essentials, such as a full uniform or other issued belongings customarily carried in one's seabag. An incompetent or simply stupid sailor is also said to be **sailing without a full seabag**.

Shut up and color

Quit complaining and just go about your make-work assignment. More emphatic: **Sierra Tango Foxtrot Uniform** (STFU)—*Shut The Fuck Up*.

Sierra hotel

NATO phonetics for SH, signifying *shit-hot*, a designation applied to a highly aggressive, enthusiastic, hard-charging aviator or, less frequently, soldier.

Skimmer puke

What a U.S. Navy submariner calls any member of a surface ship's crew. The submariner's term for the vessel itself is **target**.

Sniper check

Saluting an officer while on an active battlefield or other hostile ground is technically a requirement of military courtesy, but is in fact frowned upon since the soldier rendering the salute identifies the other person as an officer, which makes him an instant sniper target. Such a battlefield salute is therefore called a **sniper check**. Depending on the soldier and the officer, a **sniper check** may be a lapse in common sense or an accident on purpose.

Snotty

A midshipman who serves aboard a training ship.

Straight leg

An infantryman, called such because he walks everywhere. Contrast a **bent leg**, which may describe a paratrooper (who lands with legs bent at the knees) or a tanker or soldier attached to any mechanized unit (who sits, legs therefore bent).

STUMP

Acronym used by infantrymen to describe armored personnel or to indicate their presence: *Stupid Tankers Under Mortar Protection.* Tankers (along with everybody else, actually) habitually look down on infantry grunts (see **Crunchie**). This infantry acronym is their comeuppance.

SUC

Small Unit Coward: an official-sounding strictly unofficial MOS (*Military Occupation Specialty*) identifying someone as permanently deficient in guts. "What's your major malfunction, Private Smith? You changed your MOS to **SUC**?"

Swinging dick

A squared-away marine or spit-and-polish army infantryman, whose penis—in theory, at least—smartly swings, pendulum-like, to the beat of the cadence.

TESTICLES

Coined during the Vietnam War, a Special Forces acronym encapsulating the ideal characteristics of a Green Beret or other personnel assigned to special, high-risk missions: T*eam player,* E*nthusiasm,* S*tamina,* T*enacity,* I*nitiative,* C*ourage,* L*oyalty,* E*xcellence (as in professional know-how),* S*ense of humor.*

Tooth fairy

A military dentist. This medical professional traditionally gets little respect in the U.S. armed forces because of the perception that the serving dentist is a brand-new graduate of dental school, not very skilled, and eager to do no more than put in the minimum time required to repay the army, navy, or air force for financing his or her education before leaving to embark on civilian practice.

Uncle Sam's Canoe Club

Affectionate U.S. Navy name for the United States Coast Guard.

Uncle Sam's Misguided Children

An informal translation of the acronym "USMC."

Water walker

Any noncom or officer who receives the maximum rating on his or her efficiency report from both the rater and the endorser. It is generally believed that only Jesus Christ could possibly achieve such miraculous ratings—but, then, he could also walk on water.

Whale shit

That to which USMC drill instructors compare the USMC recruits in their charge, pointing out that this substance is the only thing in the universe lower than a USMC recruit.

Whip It Out

Not what *you* think it is, but, rather, a synonym for snapping a smart salute. The phrase is part of a rule-of-thumb rhyme, "When in doubt, **whip it out**," meaning that if you are unsure whether or not to salute an officer or superior in a given situation, go ahead and salute him or her—and do so smartly and without hesitation. The only thing likely to incur greater brass-plated displeasure than a failure to salute is rendering a salute that appears hesitant and half-hearted.

Without a full seabag

A sailor perceived as deficient in intellect.

Zoomie

What nonflying service members call any military aviator.

THREE

After Women
or Liquor

*Conduct Unbecoming but
Completely Understandable*

★ ★ ★

Acetate commando

A deskbound rear-echelon officer notorious for issuing aggressive commands and assigning dangerous missions.

After Women Or Liquor

Widely believed to be the actual meaning of the acronym AWOL, which officially means A*bsent* W*ith*O*ut* L*eave*. Those who reject this meaning alternatively embrace **A W**olf **O**n *the* **L**oose.

Air Start

USMC euphemism (if that is the correct term) for fellatio, which is to say a *blow* job.

Bad Paper

What you get if you fail to get an Honorable Discharge. The "bad paper" may be a "Bad Conduct" discharge, a discharge for being "Undesirable," or a "Dishonorable Discharge"—the worst that can happen short of execution by firing squad.

Ballwalking

Apparently, from time to time in a mood of youthful exuberance, male U.S. Navy and Marine officers unzip their trousers, pull out their genitals, and display them while strolling about in public. Failing to come up with an imaginative name for this activity, practitioners and observers alike have dubbed it **ballwalking**. The word entered the public lexicon in 1991, after the emergence of the infamous Tailhook Scandal, in which more than a hundred navy and marine aviators were alleged to have sexually assaulted at least eighty-seven women and engaged in other "improper and indecent" conduct (**ballwalking** included) during the 35th Annual Tailhook Association Symposium at the Las Vegas Hilton, September 8-12, 1991. For the record, the Department of Defense does not endorse **ballwalking**.

Bayonet sheet

U.S. military officers live and die—professionally—by efficiency reports (ER). Reports that are satisfactory or better will get you promoted. Those that are less than satisfactory will delay promotion, perhaps sufficiently to force a separation from the service. A strongly unsatisfactory efficiency report is grounds for immediately moving an officer out of a particular job, posting, or command. A **bayonet sheet** is such a report. It is possible that the strongly negative ER is perfectly fair and accurate; however, the phrase implies an ER framed in such a way to ensure that an unpopular officer—or one who has pissed off the wrong people—is booted. In short, the purpose of the **bayonet sheet** is to stab its subject in the gut, right where it hurts.

BCGs

"Birth Control Glasses": the heavy black horn-rim eyeglasses issued to soldiers in need of corrective lenses. Capable of instantly transforming the most suave individual into a dork, BCGs are believed to be unfailingly repulsive to the opposite sex. Typical of U.S. military practice, the armed forces stopped issuing wire-rim eyeglasses, standard for much of the twentieth century, during the late 1960s, when such eyewear had come into fashion among civilians, and issued heavy plastic Clark Kent specs thereafter.

Beltway Bandit

Synonym for a civilian military contractor, consultant, or lobbyist. The Capital Beltway is Interstate 495, which encircles Washington, D.C. Within the Beltway are the Capitol, White House, and cabinet and administrative office buildings. Outside the Beltway are the many government offices in Maryland and Virginia, most notably the Pentagon. A **Beltway Bandit** knows them all.

Big Chicken Dinner

A BCD, or B*ad* C*onduct* D*ischarge*, which is marginally better than a DD, D*ishonorable* D*ischarge*, but far short of an honorable discharge.

Boom-boom

Sex for soldiers during the Vietnam War. "Let's get into Saigon for some **boom-boom**."

Charlie's Chicken Farm

A minimum-security military prison is a Correctional Custody Facility, or CCF, or Charlie Charlie Foxtrot, or **Charlie's Chicken Farm.**

Check valve

Modern ships are full of pipes, some of which are equipped with **check valves**, which allow fluids to flow one way only. By analogy, a sailor who looks out for number one and has no consideration for others, a selfish seaman, is dubbed a **check valve.** Nothing good (say, fresh fruit at mess—always in short supply aboard ship) gets by him, and nothing good goes back to anyone else.

Churning butter

Having sex.

Cinderella liberty

Shore leave (liberty) that expires at a set time, typically midnight (when Cinderella's coach turned back into a pumpkin).

Clearing barrel

An arms safety device, the **clearing barrel** is a red barrel filled with sand and positioned anywhere soldiers are required to turn in their weapons. To verify the rifle or handgun is empty—"cleared"—before turn-in, each soldier, in line, one after the other, dry fires the weapon directly into the sand-filled barrel. By metaphoric extension, the phrase refers to any notoriously promiscuous female soldier. It is not intended as a compliment.

Crossbar Hotel, the

Military prison: in the U.S. Navy and Marines, the brig; in the other services, the stockade.

Cumshaw

The term, widely used in the U.S. Navy and Marines during World War II and still occasionally heard, derives from the Chinese *kam sia,* an archaic expression meaning "grateful thanks." Many sailors and marines served in and around China during the nineteen twenties, and the term may originally have been picked up during that period. At about the time of the outbreak of World War II, *kam sia* was slyly corrupted into **cumshaw** as a word for the bribes prostitutes working Honolulu's Hotel Street paid the local constabulary to leave them alone. Perhaps Pearl Harbor-based sailors and marines revived the old *kum sia* as "**cumshaw**" at this time or they may have simply adopted **cumshaw** directly from the prostitutes. In either case, the word describes a present, treat, or (most often) desperately needed piece of equipment that suddenly appears in a military unit even as it simultaneously and mysteriously disappears from another unit or the storage depot. Every unit had at least one **cumshaw artist**, who was expert in acquiring desired or needed items on demand and without probing questions. The spelling of the first syllable implies the sexual act, almost certainly reflecting its use among prostitutes.

Eye fuck

To stare at ("eyeball") someone. The phrase is commonly used among marines, but is heard in other service branches, too.

Feather merchant

A phrase universal throughout the U.S. military, **feather merchant** primarily refers to anyone who has a cushy noncombat assignment. This includes civilian military employees. Occasionally, the phrase is also used to describe a soldier, sailor, airman, or marine who is unusually short and slight. The word has existed outside of the military for a long time as a synonym for *loafer.* There are reports that, in a military context, the phrase originated as early as the American Revolution to describe merchants who sold feathers to the Continental Army for use in soldiers' bedding and pillows. The feathers were sold by weight, and unscrupulous **feather merchants** added rocks to the bundles. This etymology is almost certainly apocryphal, however, since the Continental Army did not supply featherbeds to common soldiers and therefore had little reason to buy feathers in bulk.

FPU

Label applied by male marines to any female marine they find reasonably attractive, which, depending on a variety of circumstances, might be any female marine. The acronym stands for F*ield* P*leasure* U*nit.*

Gundeck

In traditional U.S. Navy usage, this *verb* means to jury-rig something aboard ship—that is, to improvise rigging or make an ad hoc repair using whatever happens to be around. In more recent times, the verb usually means to fudge or falsify a record or a report. "I wouldn't risk a court martial **gundecking** that report. Just tell the truth and face the music."

Gut

Precisely the part of any port town sailors find most desirable, lined with cheap bars and fast women. Precisely the part of town the skipper declares off limits when releasing the crew for liberty.

Hooligan Navy

Of all the derogatory terms U.S. Navy sailors have invented for the U.S. Coast Guard, **Hooligan Navy** is the only one based on history. During the 1920s, when Prohibition was in full force, rejects from the other services, including the USN—men discharged as "undesirables"—were welcomed into the Coast Guard, which needed personnel to man cutters tasked with catching rum runners. Thus USCG vessels were often crewed by certified hooligans.

Kickstanded

A member of the armed forces is **kickstanded** when he or she is forced into retirement, typically for reasons of political expedience. The origin of the term is what happens to a motorcycle if its drive wheel is raised out of contact with the ground by using the kickstand: it can spin, but it can't get anywhere.

Midnight requisition

Theft by another name, the term is used exclusively when someone from one unit appropriates equipment or other goods from another unit, not for personal gain, but for the benefit of his own unit. Soldiers, sailors, marines, and airmen of a vaguely Marxist bent prefer the phrase **midnight redistribution**, as in "redistribution of wealth."

NAVY

As an acronym, this word has been made to stand for any number of things, almost universally unpleasant, including N*ever* A*gain* V*olunteer* Y*ourself* and N*eed* A*ny* V*aseline* Y*et*?

Night Ops

Sounds both glamorous and dangerous, but, on board a U.S. Navy ship at sea, is neither. The disposal of garbage is governed by any number of complex and often arduous rules, including steps to avoid detection by an enemy and steps to protect the environment. Many sailors, however, handle garbage by waiting until an odd hour of the night and simply heave it overboard when no one is looking: **night ops.**

Numb nuts

Used throughout the U.S. military, but most prevalently in the U.S. Marine Corps (and often by drill instructors), **numb nuts** is a form of address directed at anyone perceived as so hopelessly inept as to be worthless.

Compare the term to the older *numskull*, familiar in civilian use. An alternative is **scrot**, short for *scrotum.*

Passion ration

Any sexual liaison, such as in the course of a weekend pass.

Pigs in a bucket, fuck it.

A charming U.S. Navy rhyme meaning to forget about something bad, illegal, or in error you've just seen or done. The marine equivalent is **FIDO,** *Fuck It, Drive On.*

Pirate's dream

What a male sailor calls a flat-chested woman, the idea being that her small breasts are buried treasure or that she has a "sunken chest"—like a pirate's treasure chest that has gone down with a ship.

Pisscutter

This was once the universal nickname for the folding garrison cap worn by personnel in the U.S. Marines (who sometimes call it a **pisscover**), U.S. Navy, U.S. Coast Guard, and U.S. Air Force (where it is officially called a flight cap). It was first issued to U.S. Army personnel in World War I, when it was referred to as an "overseas cap," but has now been largely replaced by the beret. No one is quite sure of the etymology of **pisscutter**, though it is reported that older marines use the term to refer to any uniform article with a sharp fold, edge, or crease. The term, which is now rarely heard, may be obscurely related to another old-time alternative synonym for the garrison cap, **cunt cap**. While decidedly politically incorrect, the term is at least anatomically evocative because the original garrison cap design had a triple fold at the cap's peak, which was sewn together in a way that gapped open—suggestively to some—when worn. Present-day garrison caps lack this triple fold and anatomical effect. As with **pisscutter**, the term is rarely heard today.

Pounding (or pulling) your pud

In the civilian world, this is somewhat outdated slang for masturbating. In the military, to **pound your pud** means to stand around and do nothing; to waste time; to goof off. "Soldier, don't stand there **pounding your pud**, follow me!"

Redneck credit card

Also known as an **Arkansas credit card** or a **West Virginia credit card**, this is a simple siphon used to transfer gasoline from one vehicle to another—often without authorization.

Ropeyarn

In the old navy, this was the term for a day off to attend to such personal duties as grooming and uniform maintenance and repair. In the contemporary navy, a **ropeyarn** is time off—typically—to get laid (or make the attempt).

Shack-job

A male service member's steady girlfriend, with whom he lives off-base.

Six, six, and a kick

Maximum penalty a General Court Martial can hand down: six months forfeiture of pay, six months imprisonment with hard labor, and dishonorable discharge.

Skate

Also called a **skater**, the term is applied (often with some degree of envy and admiration) to any U.S. Navy sailor with a talent for avoiding work without detection or consequences. It is a moderate achievement to be a successful **skate** when assigned to a larger work party of fourteen men, but it is a standout achievement to prevail as a **skate** in a seven-man party. The ability to avoid work at this level is referred to as **skating golden**. Indispensable to the **skate** is the **skateboard**, a clipboard holding sheets of paper (content unimportant) that implies work yet allows the holder to stroll about the ship aimlessly and without actually doing anything.

Skivvy honcho

A marine, soldier, sailor, or airman with a reputation as a ladies' man. *Skivvies* are underwear.

Skivvy house

Brothel.

Sleeping dictionary

A female sexual partner who doubles as an informal language instructor and cultural tutor to a military advisor stationed in a foreign post.

Steam 'n' cream

Soldier term for a "massage parlor" known to offer a "happy ending" (hand masturbation) or even fellatio. This is not the same as a bordello, because the women are generally fully clothed and do not encourage—indeed, aggressively discourage—fondling, kissing, and anything else that might be mistaken for actual tenderness or affection.

Swoop

Marines use this as a noun and apply it to any weekend trip taken off base.

Taco

In the U.S. Air Force, an informal term for the "U" that appears in any report indicating "unsatisfactory" performance. Viewed in cross section, a taco is U-shaped.

Throwing hands

Engaging in a fistfight. "You and me, we got a problem. We're gonna be **throwing hands**."

Two-six-ten

Phrase used to motivate an uncooperative sailor, presaging a kick in the posterior: "It'll take two surgeons six hours to remove ten inches of my boot up your lazy ass, Seaman Jones."

Verbum sap

Short for *Verbum sapienti sat est*—"A word to the wise is sufficient." This is a dire warning cloaked in understatement. "The colonel will not appreciate your sniffin' around his fifteen-year-old daughter, private. **Verbum sap**."

WESTPAC Widow

In the U.S. Navy, "WESTPAC" stands for Western Pacific operations area. Sailors also speak of being assigned "a WESTPAC," meaning a long sea deployment to that area. This leaves many a wife ashore, some of them looking to live the life of a **WESTPAC Widow**, an absent sailor's spouse in search of extramarital sex (often with a nondeployed sailor).

FOUR

Bang-bang, Beans, Bullets, Bandages & Badguys

Fighting Words

★ ★ ★ ★

0 Dark Stupid

Any ridiculously early time to be waking up, such as 0400. Variations on this synonym for really early include **0 Early Hundred, 0 Dark O'clock,** and **0 Dark Early**.

0-Dark-30

Any time when everyone else is off duty. **0-Dark-30** is the traditional time for launching a covert operation, such as the Navy SEAL assault on the compound of Osama Bin Laden on May 2, 2011. Pronounced "zero-dark-thirty."

Alpha Bravo

An ambush.

Angel

Used in Operation Iraqi Freedom, a term for a soldier killed in combat.

Antenna farm

A major military communications center. Sometimes this is referred to as an **ant farm**.

Army Christian

A battlefield religious convert. See **Battlefield religion**.

Auger in

To crash an airplane, spiraling it into the ground much as the bit of an auger digs itself into wood. If the **augering in** is the result of a midair collision, it is often preceded by **aluminum rain**, a shower of debris falling from the sky.

Back scratching

For most of us, a pleasurable relief. For a tank commander, however, "**back scratching**" describes a defensive technique in which the crew of one tank directs raking machine gun fire against enemy infantry trying to board another (friendly) tank. To scratch a tank's back without hitting anything vital on the tank requires great delicacy and doesn't always work the way it's supposed to.

Bang-bang

What soldiers call a pistol or rifle. Really. "Soldier, field strip that **bang-bang** for immediate inspection."

Battlefield religion

The spiritual epiphany many soldiers undergo the instant they are fired upon. This is also known as a **foxhole conversion**. As the saying goes, "There are no atheists in a foxhole."

Beans

In the military, the word is more often applied to food or rations in general than it is to the particular legumes (these are known as **whistle-berries**, for their legendary tendency to produce flatulence). Indeed, **beans** is most often used in a logistical context rather than as a synonym for a meal. In planning a mission, for instance, commanders will figure what is needed in the way of **"beans and bullets"**—food rations, ammo, and other combat supplies.

Beans, Bullets, Bandages & Badguys

What combat units call administration and logistics in preparation for a battle. The preoperation document known as a Warning Order includes administrative and logistical requirements: how much rations will be required ("beans"), how much ammo ("bullets"), what types and quantities of medical supplies ("bandages"), and what provisions will be made for enemies captured as POWs ("badguys").

Bedcheck Charlie

The Korean War version of World War II's **Washing Machine Charlie**. In both cases, these were enemy aircraft with exceptionally noisy engines—usually twin-engine craft with engines deliberately desynchronized—intended to awaken, rattle, and generally harass U.S. and Allied troops by flying over an encampment or forward position in the middle of the night. The planes rarely carried out anything other than mildly destructive missions, dropping a few bombs or making a strafing run. The principal target was morale.

Believer

An enemy corpse. "Made a **believer** outta him, didn't we?"

Big Surprise, The

Who doesn't *love* surprises? Whatever *could* it be? This one is USAF pilot jargon for World War III. "Some of the old-timey Cold Warriors are still on the flight line licking their chops, just waiting for **The Big Surprise**." Pilots also use the phrase **Day One** or **Wave One** as a synonym for **The Big Surprise**. Strictly speaking, *Day One* and *Wave One* refer only to the opening military movements of a war, but, since we're talking World War III, the first movement is assumed to be tantamount to the last, and so these phrases adequately capture the whole shebang. Alternative pilot phrases for **The Big Surprise** also include **The Big Contingency** and **Round Three**.

Bigger bang for the buck

This phrase, now widely used in the civilian world, was coined during the Cold War by President Eisenhower's Secretary of Defense Charles Erwin Wilson (1953-1957) to describe the policy of investing in "strategic" (that is, thermonuclear) weapons and weapon systems rather than fully manning and equipping "conventional" (non-nuclear) forces. The idea was that, dollar for dollar, nukes provided a greater deterrent and more destructive potential. Defense Department wags insisted that the Soviet counterpart to the policy embodied in this phrase was **More rubble per ruble**.

Black Ditch Monument

What some Vietnam vets call the Vietnam Veterans Memorial, dedicated on November 13, 1982, in Washington, D.C., and designed by Yale architect Maya Ying Lin from a concept created by former infantry corporal Jan Scruggs. The somber, ground-hugging V-shaped black granite wall rises and descends into the earth and is inscribed with the names of all U.S. service members killed in the war. While most visitors consider it a moving masterpiece, others find it depressing, calling it the **Black Gash of Shame**, the **Black Ditch of the Dead**, or simply the **Black Ditch Monument**.

Bleeding edge

This sardonic variation on "leading edge" is applied to the most advanced element of an attack or assault force, which is naturally expected to absorb more casualties than those who follow behind.

Bought the farm

Got killed. Among military aviators it is widely believed that the origin of the phrase is the early policy of the U.S. Army Air Corps to reimburse farmers for crops destroyed by the crash of a misfortunate trainee. Most farmers inflated their losses, angling for the highest compensation they could get; therefore, if you got yourself killed, you "bought the farm." Other commentators believe that the "farm" refers to nothing more than the plot of land constituting the aviator's grave.

Box job

A military funeral. "Box" = coffin.

Bravo Sierra

NATO phonetic representation of something a lady of Victorian Britain would call poppycock.

Bring smoke

A request or command to direct heavy artillery fire or tactical air bombardment against an enemy position. "We need to **bring smoke** on all those hill positions now! Commence firing!"

Bug out

As a verb, to beat a hasty retreat, especially in defiance of orders or in the absence of command. As a noun (often hyphenated or spelled as one word), someone who shirks responsibility and never seems to be around when hard or hazardous work is required. **Bug out** was first used early in the Korean War, when northern forces invaded the south and overran one Allied position after another, forcing U.S. and South Korean troops to abandon their positions and withdraw south of Seoul. Although the term is now derogatory, a synonym for "cut and run," it was used during much of the Korean War as a label for the well-rehearsed process of dismantling a forward base (such as a MASH field hospital) in a process of rapid but orderly withdrawal.

Bumfuck

A fictitious name applied to any miserable duty posting. Also called **Podunk, Boonies, Nastyland**, and **Dead-letter office.**

Bust me on the surface

On board a submarine, how a subordinate might respond to a superior who insists on his obeying an order that puts the submerged boat in danger when the subordinate knows and intends to execute the proper procedure. "If I do that, we'll lose maneuvering, sir. I won't do it. **Bust me on the surface**." The meaning is, "Stop ordering me to do it, and if you want to discipline me, do it when we're out of danger—on the surface—not during a steep dive."

Chatterbox

U.S. military nickname for the United Nations Building on New York City's East River.

Co Cong

What Americans called female Viet Cong during the Vietnam War. The analogy was to a female college student: *co-ed*.

Cocked pistol

This synonym for DEFCON 1 (DEFense CONdition 1, the highest U.S. military alert level, signifying that all-out war has broken out or is imminent) is used not only informally (gallows humor being a favorite military pastime) but formally, during military exercises simulating the outbreak or imminence of thermonuclear war. Such simulations get so realistic that no one dares to utter the three syllables that constitute the phrase "DEFCON 1," lest someone, somewhere, friendly or unfriendly, mistake the exercise for the real thing and (as hyper-Texan Lyndon Baines Johnson used to drawl) decide to "maysh The Button." "**Cocked pistol**" is used instead.

Creature feature

The corpse of a battle-casualty submerged in water and that is partly decomposed or attacked by predators but is not yet sufficiently bloated to float (such corpses are **floaters**). The phrase comes from the generic name "Creature Features," of any series of horror movies or TV shows regularly broadcast on television.

Crispy Critters

Soldier's term for victims of napalm during the Vietnam War. The name was derived from a heavily advertised children's breakfast cereal by Post Cereals. The oat cereal pieces were shaped like miniature animal crackers.

Crunchie

One thing tank crewmembers call an infantryman, evoking the sound made by a human body when a tank track rolls over it. Another is **track lube**.

Death blossom

When Iraqi security forces came under attack during the Gulf War (1990–1991), Coalition soldiers noted that they either responded by running or by returning fire indiscriminately and in all directions: the **death blossom**.

Don't do nothing

This longtime and oft-repeated dictum of the U.S. Army Infantry School is both ungrammatical and grammatically ambiguous, but its message is actually quite clear: *don't just sit there, do something—even if it's the wrong thing.*

Double tap

According to professional killers, this is the most efficient way to shoot someone dead: two shots at the same aimpoint, fired in rapid succession. This is sometimes called **killing a corpse**.

Double veteran

To have sex with a woman and then kill her qualified one as a **double veteran**. The Vietnam War was an abundant source of atrocities and atrocity lore. This phrase was a product of both.

Dr. Pepper

Back in the 1940s, the marketers of the Dr. Pepper soft drink came up with an ad promoting "Dr. Pepper Time," which was defined as 10, 2, and 4 o'clock, when you were supposed to drop everything, open up a Dr. Pepper, and drink it down. The idea was driven home in a popular World War II-era radio show sponsored by Dr. Pepper and at first called "The 10-2-4 Ranch," then "10-2-4 Time." For years after the promotion and the shows were history, the numbers 10, 2, and 4 continued to appear on Dr. Pepper bottle caps, arrayed in their proper clock positions. During the Vietnam War, U.S. pilots applied the term **Dr. Pepper** to the distressingly effective North Vietnamese SAM (surface-to-air missile) tactic in which three SAMs were fired at an aircraft simultaneously, one from the 10 o'clock position (with respect to the aircraft), one from the 2 o'clock, and one from the 4 o'clock.

Droppy

Slang for a shell casing or expended cartridge, which is normally ejected (or dropped) from the weapon after firing. Also called **brass**. If you don't want evidence of your presence—other than a corpse that was once a target—you must meticulously "pick up your **droppies**" or "police your **brass**" before leaving the scene.

Embalmed beef

During the Spanish-American War (1898), soldiers were issued canned meat products that were universally unpalatable and, in some cases, dangerous or even fatal. Unscrupulous meat packers subjected spoiled beef to processing and reprocessing before canning it. At the very least, it tasted terrible. At worst, it made soldiers sick. Soldiers said it was not so much canned as embalmed: **embalmed beef**.

Eternal patrol

Submariners and their vessels lost at sea are never finally listed as "lost at sea," but as on **eternal patrol**. When the loss of individual submariners is conveyed, they are never reported as killed in action or lost at sea, but as "**Still on patrol**." All submarine forces in all national navies observe this tradition.

Expectant

Used as a noun, a casualty who is expected to die. The term was employed in field hospitals and aid stations during the Vietnam War.

Fang

Used as a verb, meaning to rebuke, upbraid, censure, or criticize mercilessly. "The sarge will **fang** you something fierce if you do that."

Fangs out

An adjective pilots themselves use to criticize any pilot (other than themselves) who is determined to score a victory in a dogfight, regardless of cost. A "**fangs out** pilot" fails to **check 6** (check his 6 o'clock—that is, look to see who's on his tail), fails to look out for others in his formation, and fails to check the status of his fuel in single-minded determination to get a kill. If he succeeds, he's a hero. If he fails, he gets himself—or some other friendly—killed.

Fine and Pleasant Misery, a

Synonym for the profession of the infantryman.

Five knots to nowhere

The speed and port of call generally assigned to ballistic missile submarines in the U.S. Navy. They are sent out on station—a classified field of criss-cross submerged sailing, awaiting the call to unleash thermonuclear Armageddon.

Flint face (or flintface)

The emotionless, inhuman expression desirable on the face of a soldier on parade or standing guard. The idea is that the face should have the appearance of stone sharp enough to cut and hard enough to strike sparks. A synonym more generally understood in civilian life is **deadpan**, although this also originated either in the military specifically or in gun culture generally. In the days of the flintlock musket, the "pan" was that part of the lock that held the primer (black powder used to set off the main charge in the barrel). An empty pan was referred to as a "dead pan," incapable of igniting a charge in the barrel, even as a **deadpan** expression is incapable of igniting emotion.

Fugazi

Fucked up, messed up, screwed up, and generally out of order. The term arose during the Vietnam War and was picked up by civilians, particularly in the cities of the U.S. Northeast, where it may also mean bogus, counterfeit, or simply fishy.

Furball

Originally, in World War I and World War II, the term was used by aviators to describe any particularly dangerous or fierce dogfight. In World War II, **furball** sometimes became **hairball**, which in turn spawned the adjective **hairy**, used to describe any dangerous close-call combat situation. After World War II, **furball** was also adopted by ground forces to describe any fierce combat encounter—or any noncombat tangle, dispute, problem, screw-up, or mess.

Gang-bang

Among professional U.S. soldiers, a **gang-bang** is mass airborne assault, especially a large-formation parachute drop. In civilian life, the term may refer either to gang rape or to a street gang fight, typically characterized by wild and reckless gunfire.

Geronimo!

If you were told that the U.S. Army paratroops of World War II adopted this famed jump/battle cry to honor the Apache warrior leader who was one of the army's most feared yet most respected adversaries in the so-called Indian Wars of the American West, you'd have no trouble believing it. In truth, the exclamation came from the mouth of Private Aubrey Eberhardt, a member of a parachute test platoon at Fort Benning, Georgia, who, in August 1940, was about to participate in a mass jump. Although this would become a staple of U.S. airborne tactics during World War II, it was being attempted for the very first time in the summer of 1940. On the evening before the jump, seeking to calm his nerves, Eberhardt went to the post movie theater with his buddies and saw the 1939 Hollywood movie *Geronimo,* with the Native American actor Chief Thundercloud in the title role. Feeling a little better after the film and a few off-post beers, Eberhardt told his comrades that the jump wouldn't be anything special after all. They replied that, on the contrary, he would be so scared he wouldn't be able to remember his own name. Eberhardt responded indignantly: "All right, dammit! I tell you jokers what I'm gonna do! To prove to you that I'm not scared out of my wits when I jump, I'm gonna yell *Geronimo* loud as hell when I go out that door tomorrow!" He did, and the cry—as it were—went viral.

Goat locker

In the U.S. Navy, the term for the chief petty officer's shipboard quarters. The origin of the term dates to the days of sail, when the CPO had charge of a goat or goats kept on board for their milk. Sometimes called **Menopause Manor**, a nickname apparently borrowed from the British Royal Navy.

Gourd

The human head, which may also be called one's **grape**. Both suggest a thing that can be pierced, crushed, or smashed quite easily. Also see **Grape**, p. 28.

Grease

During the Vietnam era, U.S. ground forces used this as a verb, meaning *kill*, as in "**Grease** the mothers!" The idea was that killing someone—*really* killing him, as in blowing him to bits—reduced the target to a puddle of grease. The M-3 submachine gun, used by the U.S. Army from 1942 to 1992 (and still in use by some other national militaries), was universally dubbed a **grease gun**. This, however, was less because it was certainly capable of **greasing** an enemy than because of its striking similarity to the auto mechanic's tool of the same name.

Haircut and manicure

Regular-army soldiers assigned to fight guerrillas often discovered that their adversaries had certain ways of doing things. This included killing people with what might be called extreme prejudice. Instead of leaving behind an identifiable corpse, for example, it is common practice among some insurgent as well as government troops ("death squads") to decapitate the victim and also remove all fingers to obliterate all evidence of individual personhood. The regulars who found such remains would remark that the victim had been given a **haircut and manicure**.

Ham and motherfuckers

During the Vietnam War, the name for a C-ration meal worse than any other. Locals, perpetually hungry, refused to accept it as a gift. An alternative term for this C-ration was **dead man's meal** because it contained apricots, widely believed to attract bullets.

Headhunting

Describes a mission with no tactical or strategic objective other than to kill as many of the enemy as possible. Typically, **headhunting** missions are undertaken to overawe and demoralize the enemy or to exact revenge for some enemy action.

Helmet fire

In air operations, this term refers to the mental deterioration—loss of coordination, difficulty making rational decisions, inability to act effectively—caused by oxygen deprivation (hypoxia) at high altitudes. Among U.S. Navy aviators, it refers to a situation in which a pilot becomes so overwhelmed by input that he suffers a loss of situational awareness (SA)—the "big picture" of everything going on around him and how he and his aircraft fit into it. The phrase is also used more generally to cover any instance of very confused thinking or actions or ideas that result from fixated or obsessive thinking. "All the captain can think about is taking that hill. He's got a **helmet fire** for that damn hill, and it's gonna get us all killed."

Hit the silk

Yes, this really is what World War II paratroopers said in reference to the jump: "Boys, time to **hit the silk**." Early parachutes were made of silk, and although nylon was soon favored, the original material remained enshrined in the phrase—much as a cornball piano player may still refer to "tickling the ivories," even though the keys are plastic.

Hollywood blast

A monthly parachute jump, performed without combat equipment or field gear, required of paratroopers to maintain their active jump status. **Hollywood blasts**, also called **Hollywood jumps**, also qualify the paratrooper for ongoing supplemental jump pay. The paratroopers themselves regard the exercises as an opportunity to show off—hence the name.

Home run

Originated in World War II and also used in the Korean War and the Vietnam War, **home run** describes a POW's escape and repatriation—a difficult and hence spectacular feat. The baseball analogy is quite thorough. Home base is one's unit or country; first base is combat, the battlefield; second base is the POW camp; third base is escape to (and internment in) a neutral nation. Only a **home run**, return to one's unit or country, scores. The odds of being tagged out between bases are, of course, high.

Hunting license

Official permission to "engage the enemy" given at the start of an assignment or mission. This is an order for offensive action. In its absence, no offensive action is to be taken—though troops are always expected to defend themselves as necessary.

IBS

In the civilian world, *Irritable Bowel Syndrome*. In the U.S. military, *Inflatable Boat, Small*—typically used by stealthy landing parties, such as Navy SEALs.

In the shit

During the Vietnam War, this phrase was used to describe any assignment to or experience in a zone of active combat. "Yeah, I was **in the shit** all right." More recently, it is being applied more specifically to suffering ambush or taking fire. "We're **in the shit now**. Call in air cover!"

Indian country

Widely used during the Vietnam War, this phrase still signifies enemy territory. It is derived from the Indian Wars in the American West during the post-Civil War period, when it was used to describe territory controlled by (generally hostile) Native American tribes.

IOTA

An unofficial designation sometimes applied to one-man suicide-bomber missions. The purpose of the term—"iota" means very small, insignificant—is to apply a formal-sounding name to the attack that actually denigrates or mocks it, dismissing such an attack as inherently insignificant and futile.

Iron rations

Emergency survival rations.

ISOFAC

In preparation for top-secret covert missions, a special ops team may be held in a secure area or building, sealed off from the world. Formally known as an "isolation facility," it is abbreviated **ISOFAC** and often referred to as **lock down** or **the box**.

JEEP/JEEPs

On board a submarine, no personnel are more important when needed than members of the Casualty Assistance Team—sailors in charge of controlling damage in the event of mishap. Because the work is often inherently dangerous, team members are called **JEEPs**: J*unior* E*nlisted* E*xpendable* P*ersonnel.*

John Wayne High School

The Special Forces and Special Operations training center at Fort Bragg, North Carolina. Point of the name: Everyone who trains there thinks he's John Wayne.

Joker

Code used by U.S. Navy aviators to signal that their aircraft is critically low of fuel—that is, running on empty.

Judas goat

Stockyards train goats to lead sheep or cattle to loading pens for transportation to the slaughterhouse or to the slaughterhouse itself. These animals are called **Judas goats** because they lead the lamb to slaughter much as Judas Iscariot betrayed Jesus (the Lamb of God) and led him to crucifixion. In the U.S. Army Air Forces of World War II, the brightly painted bomber used to guide and pace bomber formations in flight to their targets was called a **Judas goat**, because it, too, led the lambs to slaughter. The 8th Air Force lost 4,145 aircraft in the course of 10,631 missions.

KATN

Acronym for K*ick* A*ss and* T*ake* N*ames*—adopted as the unofficial motto of U.S. Army military police and also used to urge executing a mission with maximum effort.

Kiss the mistress, to

A synonym for a bull's-eye scored during rifle practice. Another synonym is **knock their spots off.** Supposedly, this expression originated when playing cards were used as targets in pistol competitions. The idea was to shoot out the "pips" or "spots" (hearts, diamonds, spades, clubs) on a card.

Kool-Aid

A Vietnam War-era term for a casualty KIA, killed in action. A popular children's drink—flavored powder mixed with water and sugar—Kool-Aid suggested a phonetic form of the letters *K* and *A*.

Laugh a minute, a

What crews of river operations in small boats (such as swift boats) called any mission that seemed at least survivable.

Life begins at 40

This phrase, a reference to a popular 1932 self-help book by Walter B. Pitkin (filmed in 1935 as a comedy starring humorist Will Rogers), was widely used by U.S. Navy submariners during World War II to mark the diving depth (40 feet) that afforded protection from most shallow-detonating depth charges of the era.

Long Pig

The flesh of a human being—when it is used as food, as in situations of extreme hunger, such as a long and desperate siege.

Maggie's Drawers

On the range, a red flag waved from the rifle pits to signify a complete miss during USMC marksmanship qualifying training. Any marine who is a really bad shot is said to "have **Maggie's Drawers**."

Mail call

There are two kinds: the one bearing letters, cards, and packages from home is always welcome; the other, in the form of incoming enemy weapons fire, never is. Why "**mail call**"? Artillery barrages are often called "packages," maybe one of which has your name on it.

Meatball

In the Pacific theater of World War II, this was the G.I.'s derogatory reference to the flag of Japan: the red "Rising Sun" starkly emblazoned on a white field—a sauce-covered meatball on a white plate. Alternative designations of this national symbol included "**flaming asshole**" and "**burning asshole**."

Mission creep

The uncanny and seemingly inevitable tendency of the assigned purpose of a program or campaign to extend beyond its planned boundaries. The classic case is the **mission creep** of the U.S. role in Vietnam, from merely "advisory" to bearing the brunt of major combat.

Nasty gram

Any curt and deliberately offensive order or directive issued by email. A communication qualifies as a **nasty gram** when it is obvious that it has been composed to offend.

Netrusion

In the new era of cyberwarfare, this is the term for inserting false data, corrupt programs, or Trojan horse spy programs into an enemy's computer network, typically by communication links. The word is a contraction of *network intrusion.* It is a cyberattack.

Nitnoy

Sometimes spelled **nitnoid** (or nit noy or nitnoi), this is a term widely used in the military community to describe anything diminutive or seemingly unimportant—but often important to some officer or bureaucrat. The word is derived from pidgin Thai and likely achieved popularity among U.S. personnel because of its resemblance to *nit* and *nitpick.*

No joy

An expression of failure, disappointment, lack of success, or a mission left incomplete. Often used by pilots who fail to locate enemy aircraft to engage. *Pilot 1*: "Good hunting?" *Pilot 2*: "**No joy**."

Nylon letdown, the

Emergency parachute ejection from a disabled aircraft. "I knew I couldn't land, so it was either **the nylon letdown** or **auger in** along with the jet."

OMGIF

Acronym for O*h* M*y* G*od*, I*'m* F*ucked*, which is essentially the obverse of **FIGMO**, F*uck* I*t*, G*ot* M*y* O*rders*. The first is an expression of despair, the second of careless abandon.

Over and out

A phrase used over military radios, but only in poorly researched Hollywood war movies. In actual practice, *over* comes after you have said something and signifies *over to you—awaiting your reply*. Only when you are finished communicating and are signing off do you say *out*. In fact, **over and out** would mean, *Over to you, but I won't hear you because I'm signing off*—which would be at best pointless and at worst quite rude.

Panty raid

A foray into enemy territory for the purpose of gathering evidence of enemy activity. The **panty raid** differs from a *reconnaissance* in that the objective is to bring back not merely a report but physical evidence of the enemy's presence, often in the form of photographs. The term is derived from the old-school college prank in which frat boys would steal the panties of coeds by "raiding" their dormitory or sorority house. This original sense of the phrase first appeared in print in 1949, and **panty raid** was used in the military beginning during the Korean War era.

Paper bullet, paper grenade

Bureaucratic paperwork, the filling out of which takes productive time away from the actual business of a soldier: combat against the enemy.

Play ball!

On ships of the U.S. Navy during World War II, the informal version of the command to commence firing on the enemy. The expression comes from the umpire's traditional signal to begin play in a baseball game.

Pucker factor

An informal gauge of the difficulty, risk, or fear-inducing capability of a given situation, task, mission, or (among pilots) aerial maneuver. The "pucker" to which the expression refers is the degree of contraction of the anal sphincter, and it ranges from a low of "loose" to a high of "tight"—as in "I'm so scared that, if I fart, I'll blow my brains out."

Ramp tramp

A medic who is a member of the team that processes newly arrived wounded, pushes the litter or gurney up the receiving ramp and into the emergency room or triage room, and into surgery. The term is also applied to any medic who processes the discharge of a patient after treatment or for transfer to another facility, such as rehab.

Ranger grave

The kind of "hasty" fighting position soldiers of a vanguard unit—such as Army Rangers—quickly dig. Affords a minimum of protection; therefore serves as shallow foxhole and a shallow grave.

Remington Raider

A United States Marine assigned to office duty. The term dates from World War II, when elite Marine Raider outfits such as Edson's Raiders and Carlson's Raiders were famous for achieving daring victories and Remington was famous for making very good typewriters.

Rice Krispies

Maggots devouring a decomposing corpse on the battlefield. Soldiers who have witnessed this spectacle report that the action of the maggots sounds like the "snap, crackle, and pop" used to advertise the Kellogg's breakfast cereal. The comparison is reinforced by the fact that each maggot vaguely resembles a grain of the truly delicious cereal.

Riki-tik

Do something as fast as possible. If you want it done faster than possible, the phrase is **mo riki-tik**. Common in the U.S. Armed Forces by World War II, **riki-tik** is derived from "Rikki-Tikki-Tavi," one of the stories in Rudyard Kipling's *The Jungle Book* (1894), in which the eponymous mongoose is capable of tremendously valiant acts performed at breathtaking speed.

RTFM

In a military increasingly technological in its orientation and mission, crossover between the worlds of computer science and warfare are inevitable. Thus the grunt and the IT professional share an acronym both use as a sovereign reply to any question requiring a tedious technical response: **RTFM**—*Read The Fucking Manual.*

Sausage side

During the first Gulf War (1990-1991), Coalition aircrews referred to a designated target area as the **sausage side**, a place where people were ground into sausage meat.

Semper fu

Slang for the USMC martial arts training program, the term conflates "Semper Fi" (the traditional Marine Corps greeting derived from the USMC motto, "Semper Fidelis"—Always Faithful) with kung fu (a traditional Chinese martial art).

Semper Gumby

An unofficial variation on the official USMC motto, "Semper fidelis"—"Always Faithful"—meaning "Always Flexible," which proclaims a quality just as essential to a marine. Gumby is the green clay humanoid Claymation character created for TV in the early 1950s and still popular today.

Shitbomb

Like death in battle, having to deal with some onerous problem impossible to resolve but requiring endless and endlessly tedious debate and discussion is an occupational hazard of life in the military service. When such an issue is suddenly brought up just before the end of an endless meeting, it is referred to as a **shitbomb**. Almost invariably, the thrower of the **shitbomb** is someone who knocks on the door, enters the meeting, drops the bomb, and then withdraws to enjoy the rest of *his* day.

Shitty Shitty Bang Bang

During the Vietnam War era, when a veteran ground soldier would swap war stories with a fellow vet, he would use this phrase as a nonchalant yet macho synonym for an armed exchange or skirmish. "I was on point, saw a shadow, heard nuthin'—until, all of a damn sudden, it was **shitty shitty bang bang**." The phrase comes from *Chitty Chitty Bang Bang,* Ken Hughes's wildly popular 1968 family movie about a flying car with a Roald Dahl screenplay based on an atypical novel by James Bond creator Ian Fleming.

Smooge

Combat pilot's term for smoke or smoke and flames rising from a target and indicating a successful hit, even in the absence of obvious wreckage and debris. The word may be a smash-up of *smog* and *smudge,* although some believe it was borrowed by U.S. fliers from an Australian word for a pass at a girl so hot that it makes her smoke + melt (that is, *smooge*) inside.

Snake eater

This is the generic name for any Special Forces type—Army Ranger, Green Beret, or Navy Seal—bestowed by ordinary service men and women.

Snoopin' and poopin'

How a marine would have described a patrol mission during the Vietnam War. The "snoopin'" is the purpose of the mission. The "poopin'" is an unwelcome side effect of time spent in a tropical jungle.

Spill the groceries, to

To sustain a severe abdominal wound, causing the intestines to be exposed.

Stans, the

Slang for the Middle Eastern and West Asian and Central Asian regions, where countries and provinces all seem to end in "stan": Afghanistan, Dagestan, Pakistan, and so on.

Stay frosty

A command among soldiers and marines to stay alert—to avoid the complacency that comes with mistakenly assuming one is in a "friendly" (secure) environment. Instead of acting warm and friendly, it is best to be frosty and wary. "Could be hostiles here, gentlemen. **Stay frosty**."

Tallyho!

Almost certainly the only word USAF fighter pilots have ever borrowed from the British fox hunting crowd. For the hunters, it is the cry elicited by the sighting of the fox and is meant to rouse the hounds, thereby setting them on the chase. For a pilot, **Tallyho!** signals sighting of the enemy. **Tallyho pounce!** means "target sighted, am in position to attack." **Tallyho heads up!** means "target sighted but unable to engage" and is used to alert one's wingman and other members of the flight or formation to the presence of the enemy. Traditionally—at least since the leather helmet days of World War I—pilots were sent into the air with the phrase "Good luck and good hunting."

Tango Uniform

NATO phonetics for the initials "TU," signifying "Tits Up," meaning dead, killed, or destroyed. "We hit the target, Sir. It's **Tango Uniform**." May be applied to people, vehicles, aircraft, buildings, or any other target. Outside of the military, certain government and police agencies also use **Tango Uniform** to indicate someone killed or something destroyed or nonfunctioning. In civilian application, however, the phrase is often sanitized as "toes up."

Tooth-to-tail ratio

An informal phrase used to describe the proportion of combat forces (tooth) to logistical and support forces (tail) in a given military formation.

Trench

The most remarkable thing about this common word used to describe the iconic fighting fortification of World War

I is its etymological longevity. World War I trenches were nasty, dirty places associated with two serious infections. Acute necrotizing ulcerative gingivitis (ANUG), a severe gum infection, was so common among soldiers of the Great War that, since then, it has been universally known as **trench mouth**. Another condition—swollen, blistered, ulcerated, and even gangrenous feet caused by continual exposure to cold and damp plus the wearing of constricting shoes or boots—is **trench foot**, which physicians sometimes call immersion foot. The condition was first recorded during Napoleon's retreat from Russia in 1812 and was a debilitating plague during World War II and the Vietnam War, but it was the World War I term that stuck. On a more positive note, the cold, damp misery of the trenches gave rise to a military-issue, water-repellant overcoat designed by the famed Burberry company with metal D-rings for the suspension of gear and equipment. It was the **trench coat**.

Truscott Trot

The rapid standard march tempo for the U.S. Army infantry introduced during the mobilization for World War II by Major General Lucian Truscott, legendary as a tough trainer of tough troops. The quick tempo was soon adopted throughout the army.

Turn-to

Dating from the age of sail and still heard in English-speaking navies, to **turn-to** is to report for a work detail or to start working. Used as an imperative verb, **turn-to** is a sharp order to get up out of one's rack and get to work.

Un-ass

To leave or move out of a station, area, or position. "**Un-ass** this position and set up five clicks up the road." Also used to urge one to get off one's ass. In either case, the idea is to get moving.

Vampire, vampire, vampire!

The call U.S. Navy aviators issue over their radios to warn of incoming air-to-air or surface-to-air missiles.

Voting machines

During the Vietnam War, U.S. soldiers sardonically referred to tanks belonging to the South Vietnamese army (Army of the Republic of Vietnam, ARVN) as **voting machines**, because they were brought out only during numerous coup d'etats in an effort to keep the current government in office, yet they never (it seemed) were available for use against the Viet Cong.

Zero Ward

Obsolete name for the area of a field hospital reserved for wounded personnel not expected to survive. These patients were given large doses of morphine and other palliatives, if available. Synonyms for the **Zero Ward** include **final encampment** and **last bivouac**. Compare **Zero-Zero Ward**, which was sometimes used to designate the area in which those with contagious diseases were quarantined when not expected to recover.

Zip

This derogatory and offensive term for any Asian surfaced during World War II and was also applied during the Korean War and the Vietnam War. That it was sometimes lengthened to **zipperhead** (usually in reference to a Vietnamese civilian) tends to lend credibility to the theory that the word derived from the zippered leather flying helmet World War II Japanese pilots wore. Nevertheless, some insist that the word is actually an acronym for *Zero Intelligence Potential*, signifying that, if captured, an Asian soldier will not crack or speak under interrogation and therefore is valueless as a source of enemy intelligence. The implication? Kill rather than capture. Even today, **zips** is sometimes heard in reference to the locals wherever one is stationed.

FIVE

Burn Before Reading

*Military Intelligence
and Other Oxymorons*

★ ★ ★ ★ ★

Absurdistan

What many U.S. military personnel who serve in Afghanistan call Afghanistan—in reference to its religious zealotry and tribalism. In 2006, Gary Shteyngart published *Absurdistan*, a bestselling comic novel. U.S. armed forces personnel seem to have adopted the term shortly after the novel appeared.

Admiral's Gestapo

An unsympathetic term for the Naval Investigative Service (NIS).

Airdale

In contrast to Airedale, a terrier breed originating in the Airedale region of Yorkshire, England, an **airdale** is what nonflying military personnel call a pilot or other aircrew. The term, mildly derogatory, has long been used in both the U.K. and U.S. military and was so common by the Cold War era that when the Central Intelligence Agency (CIA) purchased a civilian airline, Civil Air Transport (CAT), for covert operations in 1951, it hid its acquisition through another CIA shell company called American Airdale Corporation—an action that passed for a sly inside joke by an agency little known for its sense of humor.

Aunt Minnie

A photograph taken by a civilian—an amateur, a tourist, or a photojournalist—that happens to reveal material of interest to military intelligence. The idea is that the photographer intended nothing more than to portray his "Aunt Minnie" but, in the process, captured background images of reconnaissance value. Photo interpreters generally crop the old lady out of the picture before passing it on to higher headquarters.

Biographical leverage

A G-2 (intelligence) doublespeak synonym for *blackmail,* which might be used to extract information or motivate a subject to do something disagreeable to him but useful to investigators. Those who occupy the innermost ring of the inner intelligence circle (or want to suggest that they do) shorten the phrase to **bio lever**. "We might be able to get the guy to spill if we can get a nice juicy **bio lever** on him."

Blue feature

Any body of water as seen on a military map—so called because it is colored blue.

Blue on blue contact

Euphemism for a friendly fire incident, also known as fratricide. In war games and other combat simulations, the "blue force" is the friendly force and the "red force" the enemy. Blue is also the color of full-dress uniforms of all the U.S. services.

Body snatchers

The term may be applied to soldiers or civilian operatives assigned to capture enemy personnel for interrogation, or to Mortuary Affairs (known in the U.S. Army as Graves Registration before 1991) troops (or others) assigned to recover battlefield KIA following an engagement. The latter are also called **ghouls**.

Burn Before Reading

Everyone who's ever watched a spy movie is familiar with the top-secret document stamped *Burn After Reading.* GIs imagine that, at the very *uppermost* upper echelons, privileged personnel deal daily with documents so highly classified that they are stamped **Burn *Before* Reading.** The nature of military logic (so-called) is so intimately familiar to troops that the absurd phrase seems to them very nearly plausible.

Candy

The cash contents of a secret slush fund, which is used to finance covert operations without leaving an accounting trail for whistleblowers and congressional committees to follow.

Canine 'n' Equine Extravaganza

This is a tongue-in-cheek inflation of the more familiar **dog 'n' pony show**, which is a more-or-less elaborate presentation made to top military brass or leaders in civilian government to promote a desired military program, initiative, or operation or to pry loose funding for a coveted piece of military hardware.

Cat skinner

A service member, officer or enlisted, who is especially skilled at thinking outside the box in order to attain apparently impossible objectives, to leverage scant resources, or simply to get ahead. The phrase comes from the old saw about there being "more than one way to skin a cat."

Comics

What soldiers call any map or maps prepared by military intelligence (MI). Variants include **comic book** and **funny papers**. In part, the term is a sardonic comment on the perceived (in)accuracy of the map, but it is also a reference to the many colorful symbols usually included on the document.

Crypter

A military cryptographer or cryptanalyst; sometimes spelled *cryper* or *cripper*. Not to be confused with **crypto**, which could be used as an abbreviated form of *cryptographer,* a shorthand reference to a cryptography department or section, or, applied to a person, as an expression of distrust because the subject is known to disguise his motives and true feelings; in this sense, a **crypto** is a sneak.

Delta Sierra

"DS," standing for D*umb* S*hit.* This signal was sometimes transmitted in the U.S. Navy to convey extreme disapproval of a misguided action, an error, or the poor execution of an order. It was considered the exact opposite of the signal **Bravo Zulu**, which signifies "Well Done." While **Bravo Zulu** is still used in the navy, **Delta Sierra** has been dropped. Sailors apparently no longer do stupid things.

Disneyland

What U.S. Marine recruits called the 3d Recruit Training Battalion, Recruit Training Regiment, at USMC Recruit Depot, Parris Island, South Carolina, during the 1960s. In part, of course, this was pure irony since marine recruit training is pure hell. Yet it was also an acknowledgment that the three-story ("three-deck") barracks here were brand new, in contrast with the very dated facilities elsewhere on Parris Island. 1st Battalion was nicknamed Frontier Land, but when it came to 2d Battalion, the marines left Disneyland altogether and dubbed it "The Twilight Zone."

File 13

The office wastebasket. The term is related to both **circular file** (a synonym for wastebasket common in both the military and the civilian spheres) and, most likely, the World War II-era regulation governing "Active Duty Enlisted Administrative Separations for Unsatisfactory Performance," called AR 635-200 section 13. A soldier discharged as subpar was said to have been "given a Section 13," in effect discarded.

Five O'Clock Follies

During the Vietnam War, this was the term used for the official daily briefing delivered mainly for the benefit of the mostly U.S. press. It was characterized by wild optimism and exaggerated body counts of enemy troops. During the first Gulf War of 1990–1991, the customary daily briefing was referred to as **Evening Prayers**.

Fort Fumble

The Pentagon. Also known as the **Five-Sided Squirrel Cage**.

G, The

The government of the United States—in the sense of Big Brother, ultimate authority, and faceless bureaucracy.

GCE

The ever-patient instructor (usually in the U.S. Navy) softly mutters this acronym to a student exhibiting complete failure to understand anything he has been taught. It stands for *Gross Conceptual Error* and indicates stupidity of the most profound kind.

GOBI

General Officer's Bright Idea—a useless, impractical, counterproductive, heavily bureaucratic directive "inspired" by a remark casually tossed off by a general (usually at a briefing) and invariably assigned to you for execution.

Great Mistakes

The sailor's name for Great Lakes Naval Training Center north of Chicago on Lake Michigan. The "mistake" at the root of the name is the fact that the U.S. Navy chose to close its two other training facilities, in sunny and warm San Diego, California, and sunny and warm Orlando, Florida, leaving only Chicago and its lakefront, which are sunny and warm maybe four months out of the year.

Head Shed (also spelled Hed Shed)

Marine Corps name for a headquarters or command post—but note that **head**, in the Marines and the U.S. Navy, is the designation for latrine.

Headquarterism

This term, which was apparently originated in the Union army during the Civil War, describes an aloof and removed attitude in a unit's command and staff that presumably results from the physical remoteness of the headquarters from the front lines. History's "great captains" always took pains to avoid **headquarterism** by frequently touring front-line positions and insisting that their staff officers do the same. General George S. Patton Jr. was particularly famous for this, and was always eager to show his troops that a "general could get shot at."

HIC

Acronym variously interpreted as H*ead* *i*n *C*louds and H*ead* *i*n *C*oncrete. It is applied to commanders who stubbornly insist on manifestly impractical and ineffective courses of action.

Hindquarters

Headquarters. This may have been derived from a story widely circulated through the Union army in 1862 that the notoriously pretentious and unpopular Major General John Pope made it a practice to preface all his written orders with the phrase "Headquarters in the Saddle." Some wit (no one knows who) remarked that this precisely described the general's chief weakness as a commander: he established his headquarters where his hindquarters should have been.

Hurry up and wait

A phrase popularized during World War II, it is universally regarded (at least among enlisted personnel) as the unofficial standing order of the U.S. military. Often, the phrase is used as a synonym for command inefficiency as perceived from the point of view of the grunt.

IBM

Civilians understand this as the initials of International Business Machines, but USN sailors recognize it as a label for any shipmate who has flunked out of a specialty school and will therefore be deployed as "undesignated"—in other words, an I*nstant* B*oatswain's* M*ate,* the jack of all trades on any deck. *BM* is the official abbreviation for Boatswain's Mate. An *Instant* Boatswain's Mate (**IBM**) is constituted, like any other instant commodity, by just adding water: in other words, shipping out to sea.

Jock Strap Medal

The name general military and military intelligence personnel give to decorations awarded to active members of the CIA. Unlike conventional military decorations, which are displayed proudly on one's chest, "the Company" hangs on to the decorations it awards until after the agent retires. The joke is that the only place an active agent *could possibly* pin his medal is on his jock.

Lima Lima Mike Foxtrot

Used in radio communication, the NATO phonetic acronym for *Lost Like a Mother Fucker*, which is really, really lost.

Mind candy

Derogatory term for a wildly impractical idea, a fantasy. "PFCs don't end up as chairmen of the Joint Chiefs of Staff, but that is a very tasty piece of **mind candy**, my friend."

Naked Fanny

During the Vietnam War, the U.S. Air Force maintained a base in Nhakon Phanom, Thailand, just across the Mekong River from Laos. Used as a center for communications and electronic warfare, the covert base was universally referred to as **Naked Fanny.**

National Joke Factory

A synonym for the United States Congress common in military circles ever since the humorist Will Rogers (1879–1935) came up with it in the early 1930s.

Nose count

A means of arriving at a decision without having to take personal or command responsibility for the decision. Instead of assessing a situation, deciding on a course of action, and ordering that action, a (typically junior) commander may poll peers and subordinates, solicit consensus, then initiate the action. This process is known as a **nose count**. While there is nothing inherently wrong—or unmilitary—with soliciting advice before making some decisions, evading responsibility is both frowned upon and quite common.

Nuclear waste

Sailors who wash out of prestigious training programs to qualify them for service on board nuclear-powered vessels—submarines or aircraft carriers—are referred to by this less than charitable name.

Octopus, the

The Department of Homeland Security, so nicknamed by the military because a) it has its tentacles in everything and b) it proposes to defend the nation with a never-ending stream of bureaucratic ink.

OGA

Acronym for *Other Government Agency,* by which is meant the National Security Agency (NSA), the Defense Intelligence Agency (DIA), or the Central Intelligence Agency (CIA)—all too secretive to admit involvement in anything in which they are most certainly involved.

Pig looking at a wristwatch

An evocation of the bewilderment of incompetence, this phrase is sometimes used to describe a leader at any level—but typically a squadron or platoon leader—who is out of his or her depth and is in a situation of utter incomprehension and mental paralysis.

Pins in the map syndrome

A habit of military mismanagement characterized by attempting to substitute quantity of resources for quality thereof, as when a commander addresses a tactical deficiency in the field not by changing tactics but merely by sending in more troop units—whose arrival on the scene is indicated by inserting more colored pushpins into the map posted on the headquarters wall.

Pocket litter

In preparing an agent to infiltrate enemy territory, spymasters furnish him or her with personal effects of the type that is normally found in the pockets, wallets, and purses of a person in a particular place. This so-called **pocket litter** will make the agent appear like any other (enemy) citizen.

Polish a turd

Describes any attempt to make the best of a bad situation or present an inferior product or result as acceptable. This is widely used in all the armed services and frequently heard in the halls of the Pentagon.

Pyhooya!

Uttered in imitation of the trooper's outcry of enthusiasm, affirmation, or approbation, Hooah! (or Oorah! in the Marine Corps), **Pyhooya!** is actually an acronym signifying *Pull Your Head Out Of Your Ass* and is therefore an outcry of disgust, disagreement, or disapprobation. In the U.S. military, this passes for irony.

Rectal defilade

In classic military parlance, *defilade* is the use of natural or artificial obstacles to shield or conceal oneself or one's position from hostile observation and fire. By extension, the phrase *rectal defilade* describes any word or deed intended to cover your ass. "The major's asked for three reports: a report, a report on the report, and a report auditing the report on the report. Now *that* is what I call a **rectal defilade**."

Rectal-cranial inversion

To have one's head up one's ass.

Screw the pooch

In the U.S. Air Force, a synonym for making a big and usually public mistake, such as, say, wrecking your aircraft. "You really **screwed the pooch** with that landing. Jet will be out of service for a week." Reportedly, the phrase was first used in the early 1960s, during NASA's *Mercury* manned space program, introduced into the program by John Rawlings, who helped design the astronauts' space suits. Rawlings imported it from his alma mater, Yale University—albeit in its original form, which used a more emphatic word for "screw" and had its origin in a joke ending in a punch line that has an inept lover somehow missing his lady and inadvertently having sex with her dog. Which is a *really* stupid mistake.

Variants (mostly U.S. Navy) include **pound the pooch, pop the puppy,** and **hump the bunk**. When used in an aeronautical context, any of these terms imply disaster. In other contexts, they may cover a wide range of screwups, from relatively minor and embarrassing to pressing the button that triggers thermonuclear Armageddon.

Soap chips

As part of a PSYOPS ("psychological operations") dis-information mission, agents may plant letters and greeting cards from an enemy's home country on corpses and battle wreckage for the purpose of demoralizing troops. Typically, the material is sentimental in nature—"soft soap" stuff—often also implying the impending infidelity of wives and sweethearts. **Soap chips** may be fabricated or taken from enemy casualties.

Soup sandwich

A totally fouled-up situation. A refined variation includes **split-pea on rye**, and a less refined variation is **shit sandwich**. None of the three is appealing, which is, of course, the point.

Spaghetti chart

A flow chart or diagram intended to simplify the explanation of a process or the structure of an organization, but that only makes it appear even more complicated. In other words, a prime example of military enlightenment.

Think purple, to

Imperative that instructs—indeed, implores—leaders of units from different service branches (army, navy, marines, air force) to combine their resources in a collaborative or coordinated action. As when you mix a number of paint colors together, blending the branches' different-colored uniforms will yield one shade of purple.

Tocroach (or TOCroach)

TOC is an acronym denoting T*actical* O*perations* C*enter,* the operational headquarters of a combat commander, where both intelligence and operations planning take place. Typically, the *TOC* is sheltered from frontline combat—and for this reason is sometimes called the **TOC Mahal,** an allusion to the luxurious Taj Mahal, although, typically, the TOC is a bunker or so-called bombproof. Because of its quasi-subterranean nature, one who works in the TOC is derogatorily referred to as a **Tocroach**, like the cockroach, a denizen of dark seclusion who is frightened of bright light. Also see **Fobbit**.

WAG

USMC acronym signifying W*ild-Assed* G*uess.*

SIX

Broken Arrows and Spastic Plastic

Language Built to the Highest Military Specs

★ ★ ★ ★ ★ ★

Angel track

During the Vietnam War, armored personnel carriers (APCs) were sometimes pressed into service as improvised aid stations to treat the wounded. Because the APC had tank tracks rather than tires, the vehicle thus used was called an **angel track**.

Army Lawn Dart

Soldier's nickname for the UH-60 Black Hawk helicopter, sincerely believed by many troops absolutely incapable of remaining airborne for any length of time. Alternative name, **Crash Hawk.**

Army proof

Used by personnel of the United States Air Force as a synonym for foolproof, the term is applied to any device any idiot can operate or any explanation any idiot can understand.

ASVAB waiver

What any exceptionally dimwitted, hapless, or inept service member is said to possess. The Armed Services Vocational Aptitude Battery—ASVAB—is a multiple choice diagnostic exam administered by the United States Military Entrance Processing Command (USMEPCOM) to determine eligibility for admission to the military. Currently, the U.S. Army requires an ASVAB of 31 or higher (out of a possible 100) for high school graduates. There is no such thing as an "ASVAB waiver," but it would be difficult to persuade most soldiers, sailors, airmen, or marines of this fact.

Battle rattle

Fully equipped for combat. The rhyming slang phrase is applied to the individual soldier who is properly loaded down with his or her combat gear. The phrase is often extended to **full battle rattle**. "I'm ready for it. **Full battle rattle**." Full personal combat gear as of the twenty-first century amounts to some fifty pounds' worth of Kevlar, chemical warfare protection, ammunition, and weapons.

Big green tick

The ALICE (*A*ll-purpose *L*ightweight *I*ndividual *C*arrying *E*quipment) system was adopted by the U.S. Army in 1973 as a means of carrying—well—equipment, including either a medium or large LC-1 field pack. The large pack, capable of carrying many heavy things, was dubbed the **big green tick**. Marching with as much as eighty pounds on your back was notoriously unpleasant, and so the phrase came to describe anything unpleasant, uncomfortable, or otherwise burdensome. "My mother-in-law is a **big green tick**." The phrase is not to be confused with **Big Green Dick**, which is a synonym for the U.S. Army administrative bureaucracy and may be used on any occasion but is typically reserved for those occasions on which the bureaucracy has crapped on you, which is pretty much on any occasion. The fact of the matter is that the **Big Green Dick** is a **big green tick**. (The ALICE system has been phased out. The **Big Green Dick** has not.)

Bitchin' Betty

In many U.S. military operational aircraft, computer-generated warnings are delivered in a synthesized female voice. For instance, if an aircraft descends below a preset altitude, the pilot will hear "Altitude, altitude" repeated until the situation is remedied or the aircraft **augers in**. Both the warning system and the voice are familiarly referred to as **Bitchin' Betty**. Occasionally, for the sake of variety, **Naggin' Nancy** is used instead.

Boondockers

This has been a familiar synonym for ankle-high military rough-out leather combat and work boots since the late nineteenth century, when American soldiers tramping through the jungles of the Philippines (during the Spanish American War and the so-called Philippine Insurrection that followed) borrowed it from the Tagalog word *bundok*. Formally, *bundok* means "mountain," but Filipinos apply it colloquially to any rural area. Eventually, **boondockers** was applied not only to the short work boots, but to any boots, military or civilian, suitable for travel in rough country and also to the country itself. **Boonies** is now familiar to describe any remote rural location, and the term **boonie hat** is what soldiers call the "Hat, Camouflage (Tropical Combat) Type II," first authorized in 1968. Floppy, with a wide brim, it is sometimes also called a bush hat.

Bouncing Betty

While this may sound like the kind of high-spirited lass soldiers far from home hanker after, it was neither a girl nor anything a soldier wanted to encounter during World War II. Officially known as a German S-mine (for *Schrapnellmine, Springmine,* or *Splittermine*), the **Bouncing Betty** was a "bounding" antipersonnel mine developed in the mid-1930s and used by German forces in World War II. The S-mine was a metal cylinder about five inches tall and four inches in diameter, with a steel rod protruding from the top. This was the trigger. The mine was buried with the trigger upright. When a soldier stepped on the trigger, a black powder charge blasted it two to four feet in the air. A time-delay fuse ignited the main TNT charge a half second later, creating an explosion at just the right height to kill or injure a number of troops. To make the blast even more deadly, the TNT was packed together with 360 steel balls, steel rods, or jagged shrapnel. **Bouncing Betty** was not only deadly, but created terror in any group of soldiers who encountered it.

Broken arrow

What the U.S. Air Force calls an accident—typically an airplane crash—involving a nuclear weapon. If this quaintly low-tech expression fails to dispel blinding-flash visions of Armageddon, the USAF will oblige with another, **bent spear**, which means exactly the same thing.

BUFF

A weapon that's been around as long as the mighty Boeing B-52 Stratofortress—It first flew on April 15, 1952, was last manufactured in 1962, but is scheduled to remain in service until 2045!—deserves a grudgingly affectionate acronym. **BUFF** stands for *B*ig *U*gly *F*at *F*ucker, the last element of which is sanitized to *Fellow* in polite (that is, civilian) company. The **BUFF** is so big that it is often referred to as an **aluminum overcast** as it passes overhead. Members of "the B-52 community" (as they call themselves) have a saying: "You may not be in your father's air force, but you *may* be in your father's airplane."

Bull Shit Bomber

The value of PSYOPS—psychological operations, or psychological warfare—has long been recognized, but the propaganda arsenal has never gotten a lot of respect, even from those assigned to manage and deploy it. Thus the EC-130E version of the ubiquitous Lockheed C-130 Hercules cargo transport, modified to drop propaganda leaflets and make radio broadcasts during the 1990–1991 Gulf War, was rarely called by its official name, "Commando Solo," but more frequently dubbed the **Bull Shit Bomber**.

Bummer bird

This unofficial designation could be applied to any aircraft transporting troops to the Vietnam theater of operations, but was most frequently used to refer to the many civilian airliners chartered for such transport. "Bummer" was slang closely associated with the 1960s—height of the Vietnam War—and referred to anything bad, unfortunate, or negative.

D^3

Pronounced "D cubed," this is extraordinarily succinct shorthand for a "D*rop-*D*ead* D*ecision*"—that is, a decision by military or (more often) civilian leaders to summarily cancel the development of a proposed weapons system. "The Really Big Gun? Not gonna happen. The Appropriations Committee handed down a D^3."

Dain Bramaged

Sailors' nickname for USS *Bainbridge* (DDG-96), an *Arleigh Burke*-class guided missile destroyer commissioned on November 12, 2005.

Dash Ten

Shorthand designation for any operator's manual for any item of U.S. Army hardware. The term is derived from the "-10" that serves as a suffix to the main number of the manual, such as *Operator's Manual for 2-½-Ton, 6x6, M44A3 Series Trucks (Diesel)*, which is Army TM 0-232-386-10.

Dog

On board U.S. Navy vessels, watertight doors are secured with one or more pivoting latches called **dogs.** The word may be used as a noun to describe such a latch or as an imperative verb when one orders another to turn the latch to secure a watertight door: "Close that door and **dog** it!" The mess and recreation areas of some modern USN ships feature soft-serve ice cream machines, which have also been dubbed **dogs.** While there is no connection between the appearance or function of the **dog** latch and the ice cream machine, there *is* a strong resemblance between how the machine dispenses a mound of soft chocolate ice cream and what a dog dispenses from his nether regions in the course of a morning's walk.

Dope(s) on a rope

A rope, with one or more U.S. Marines attached, let down from a hovering helicopter to insert marines into a jungle or other place unsuitable for landing. The idea is that you have to be a dope to allow anyone to do this to you. Noted boxing photojournalist George Kalinsky may have had the phrase in mind when he reportedly gave Muhammad Ali's trainer and cornerman Angelo Dundee the idea for the tactic Ali used against George Foreman in 1974 to force him to exhaust himself with futile punches: "Sort of a dope on the ropes, letting Foreman swing away but, like in the picture, hit nothing but air." The familiar phrase describing the tactic, "rope-a-dope," was coined by Ali publicist John Condon. The less pejorative USMC term for **dope on a rope** is **spy rigging**.

Dustbin

Term for the belly-mounted ball turret on a heavy bomber in the World War II U.S. Army Air Forces. All the equipment, dirt, and detritus shaken loose in flight and by enemy flak and gunfire damage typically found its way into the ball turret, which was the lowest point on the fuselage. Fighting in a **dustbin** added to the misery of existence in the ball turret, which was cramped and required the gunner to assume something like a fetal position, and which was exposed to the worst effects of enemy fire. Not infrequently, a damaged aircraft would have to make a wheels-up belly landing. If, for some reason, the ball turret hatch could not be opened, the gunner would be crushed in the crash landing.

EB Green

As any do-it-yourselfer knows, there are few things that can't be fixed—at least for a certain portion of the foreseeable future—with duct tape judiciously applied. U.S. Navy submariners get their duct tape special from the Groton, Connecticut, boatyard of Electric Boat, which builds most USN nuclear subs. The "EB" stands for Electric Boat, of course, and "Green" is the color of the utility-grade tape. In extreme emergencies, submariners resort to **EB Red**, an even heavier-duty form of the fix-it-all-for-a-while standby.

Ed's Motel

An acronym known only to members of the U.S. Navy's filmmaking unit, it stands for Ed*itorials,* Mo*tion Picture and* Tel*evision Department.*

Flak bait

World War II synonym for a glider, also known as a **canvas coffin**.

Flaming asshole

U.S. Air Force slang for the use of a jet fighter's afterburner or afterburners to achieve "full military power"—

maximum speed used in dogfights and other critical operations. Going to afterburners produces a spectacular jet of flame from the aircraft's exhaust.

Flavor extractor

A piece of equipment those who serve aboard U.S. Navy vessels believe is standard in every galley, its express purpose to render food flavorless. Although all U.S. Navy administrators vehemently deny the existence of the **flavor extractor**, it should be noted that none of them have ever actually eaten shipboard food.

Four acres of Sovereign United States Soil

A modern *Nimitz*-class aircraft carrier, the dimensions of which are 1,092 feet long by 252 feet wide: 275,184 square feet, which actually comes to six and a third acres.

Glad Bag

A body bag during the Vietnam War era. The term is derived from Glad brand trash and food-storage bags, which were introduced in the 1960s as a substitute for paper bags.

Golden rivet

Legend has it that every U.S. Navy ship is launched with a commemorative **golden rivet**, like the Golden Spike that commemorated the joining of the Union Pacific and Central Pacific railroads into a single transcontinental line in 1869. Does anyone actually believe this? You'd have to tear down every ship to disprove it.

Good training

Any mishap, mistake, or bad idea that actually doesn't get anyone killed or court martialed. "Taking that shortcut through the live-fire range was **good training**, Sarge."

G-ride

Informal U.S. military term for any civilian vehicle bearing U.S. government license plates. *G* stands for government, and *ride* is familiar slang for a car.

Hangar queen

Derisive term for a supermodern, superexpensive aircraft that spends most of its time in the hangar undergoing repairs. Sometimes, the term is used to refer to *any* airplane with a record of malfunction. In extreme conditions and in remote airfields, such craft may be used primarily as a source for replacement parts, presumably on the assumption that the problem with the machine is not in its constituent parts but in how they function—or fail to function—together.

Happy suit

The body armor worn by the modern U.S. soldier, especially in Afghanistan and Iraq. The full **happy suit** consists of antiballistic ceramic plates, Kevlar drapes, and a fire-resistant uniform, over which shoulder and knee pads are fitted.

Hatch

What marines call any door, whether on board a ship or on dry land. Sailors, in contrast, understand that, whereas an opening in a *horizontal* deck is a **hatch**, a *vertical* opening in a bulkhead is a door.

Hawespipe

On board a ship, the steel or iron pipe in the bow through which the anchor cable chain passes. To "have come up through the **hawespipe**" is to have risen through the navy ranks from the bottom to a position of authority. In other contexts throughout the U.S. military, **hawespipe** is a reference to the human rectum: "Stick it in your **hawsepipe** and take a hike."

Heat tab

C-ration field stoves were heated by burning a blue tablet of Trioxin, which soldiers and marines called a **heat tab**. If, for some reason, Trioxin wasn't available, a *small* piece of C-4 plastic explosive could be used. Not surprisingly, it created a hotter flame, which was especially useful if you were in a hurry. The downside came with using a little too much, which would explode.

Hillbilly armor

During Operation Iraqi Freedom, when it became apparent that the greatest danger to U.S. forces came from improvised explosive devices (IEDs), units scrambled to weld steel plates to their inadequately armored vehicles in a desperate bid for added protection. The ugly result was dubbed **hillbilly armor**.

Housewife

Introduced during the Civil War, the **housewife** was a small sewing kit consisting of needle, thread, and patches (and, later, a needle threader as well), so that enlisted personnel could repair their own uniforms. Officers had orderlies to do this work and therefore had no need of a **housewife**. The kit was issued through World War II.

Idiot bomb

Name U.S. military personnel applied to a Japanese suicide, or kamikaze, rocket plane patterned after the German V-1 "Buzz bomb," but designed to be piloted on a one-way trip. This guided missile was about twenty feet long and carried a 2,460-pound explosive payload. Developed late in World War II, it saw very limited service and was far less effective than the conventional aircraft kamikaze pilots flew on suicide missions.

Ink stick

United States Marine Corps term for a pen.

Iron bomb

Old-school aircraft ordnance dropped on a target: a **dumb bomb**, as opposed to a cutting-edge smart bomb, which is electronically and remotely guided.

Jesus nut

On a military helicopter, the name for the main rotor-retaining nut—basically, the one piece of hardware that keeps the rotor from flying off the machine. If that nut fails, only Jesus can help you (and not very much).

LHO

This acronym, signifying *Large Heavy Object*, is applied to any piece of major machinery deemed absolutely critical by higher command and absolutely useless by those who actually operate—or have to move—it.

L-Pill

Designation for the legendary (but very real) "Lethal Pill" issued to clandestine operatives who were presumed to prefer suicide to capture and subsequent interrogation by torture. During World War II, the L-Pill was an ampule of thin glass covered in thin rubber and filled with potassium cyanide or other liquid cyanide preparation. It was self-administered by biting down and breaking the glass, thereby releasing the poison into the mouth.

Luggage tag

The term may be applied to a Field Medical Card tied to a wounded patient's chest to indicate details of the injury and any treatment or drugs administered. Alternatively, **luggage tag** may refer to the toe tag used to identify corpses either in the morgue or awaiting transportation thereto.

Magic smoke

According to highly trained USN technicians, this is the substance that actually makes all electronic gear on naval vessels work.

Mobile Chernobyl

This is the nickname conferred on USS *Enterprise* (CVN-65), the world's first nuclear-powered aircraft carrier. Commissioned on November 25, 1961, *Enterprise* was inactivated in 2012. The explosion at the Chernobyl nuclear power plant occurred on April 26, 1986, killing thirty-one people outright and judged by some authorities to have caused 985,000 "premature" cancer deaths between 1986 and 2004. Patriotic sailors who objected to invoking a Russian nuclear disaster to describe an American ship could avail themselves of another popular nickname for CVN-65, **Quarter-Mile Island**, a reference to *Big E*'s length—1,123 feet, approaching a quarter mile—and the homegrown near-meltdown at the Three-Mile Island nuclear power plant near Harrisburg, Pennsylvania, on March 28, 1979.

NEACP

Pronounced "kneecap," this is an acronym for the National Emergency Airborne Command Post, originally flown by aircrew of the Strategic Air Command (SAC) and now by Strategic Command (STRATCOM), which serves as the airborne command headquarters for the president of the United States, the secretary of defense, and other designated staff in the event of nuclear war. The actual aircraft is a Boeing E-4, an electronic warfare modification of a standard Boeing 747-200, with the airframe modified to enhance survivability. Four of these aircraft are maintained and flown, under STRATCOM, by 1st Airborne Command and Control Squadron of the 55th Wing out of Offutt Air Force Base near Omaha. The NEACP E-4 was introduced in 1974 and is currently scheduled to be retired in 2015.

NFG

Letters emblazoned on tags applied to NonFunctioning Gear in the navy and air force. Sailors and airmen believe the acronym stands for No Fuckin' Good.

Nine yards

The length of a complete standard .50-mm machine gun ammo belt: twenty-seven feet. To feed the gunner the entire belt was to give him (or the enemy target) "the whole nine yards"; hence the popular expression for giving, getting, or doing absolutely everything.

Paper assholes

As irrefutable evidence that military personnel are capable of inventing demeaning names for absolutely everything, consider **paper assholes**, which any school supply or office supply store calls "gummed reinforcements," the stick-on paper rings intended to keep the holes in loose-leaf paper from tearing in ring binders.

Plastic brains

A preflight or postflight check list. These documents were typically mounted on a *plastic* kneeboard attached to the upper leg of a pilot's flight suit for ready reference. Nowadays, checklists are computerized and, when need-ed, are called up on a screen in the digital "glass cockpit" of a modern aircraft. Nevertheless, the name has stuck, at least among military aviators.

Queer

Not quite what you think. In the U. S. Navy, it is the nickname for the Grumman EA-6 Prowler electronic warfare aircraft, which features double-stacked side-by-side seating to accommodate a pilot and three crew member ECMOs: electronic countermeasures officers. While the navy has its **queer**, the U.S. Air Force recognizes the existence of **queertrons**—the generic term for misbehaving electrons on which otherwise inexplicable avionics (flight instrument) malfunctions are blamed. Compare **Queer** on p. 87.

Ronson

In World War II, the tanker's nickname for the M-4 Sherman medium tank, workhorse of U.S. armored units. Relatively lightly armored and running on super-flammable gasoline instead of less-volatile diesel fuel, the Shermans had a lamentable tendency to burst into flame whenever hit by an enemy round, regardless of caliber.

Crews grimly appropriated the ad slogan of the Ronson Cigarette Lighter Company, which proudly boasted of its products: "They light up every time."

Sherwood Forest

The missile compartment of U.S. Navy guided missile submarines (SSBNs) consists of a dense array of launch tubes resembling a forest of trees, which might as well be the preserve of Robin Hood, his merry men, and the sheriff of Nottingham: **Sherwood Forest**.

Sky blossom

A parachute, fully deployed—and a lot more romantic-sounding than this alternative: **falling-down umbrella**.

Spastic plastic

What the infantryman calls the M-16, primary service rifle of the U.S. armed forces since the Vietnam War. The construction of the weapon incorporates a significant number of plastic elements to reduce weight, and many 1960s-era soldiers, accustomed to the weighty M-1 Garand, which had been the ubiquitous service rifle from 1936 to 1957, found the M-16 flimsy and toylike. They dubbed the weapon the **MTR** (*Mattel Toy Rifle*). The name of this famous American toymaker (founded in 1945 and today the world's largest maker of toys) was also applied to the U.S. Army's TH-55A Osage helicopter, manufactured by Hughes Aircraft. The diminutive two-seater light-training aircraft (produced from 1961 to 1983) was usually painted bright orange, giving it a sufficiently toylike appearance to merit the moniker **Mattel Messerschmitt**.

Tank

The word is so familiar to us as the name for a tracked, armored fighting vehicle that we don't think much about it. But consider: What does such a vehicle have to do with a word that usually describes nothing more or less than a container for water or other liquids? To answer that, we first have to answer why this quintessential *land* fighting vehicle was initially developed not by an army but by the British Royal *Navy*.

In fact, early in World War I, a number of forward-looking British Army officers unsuccessfully lobbied the

War Office to begin developing armored vehicles based on the caterpillar tractor already in use in various civilian applications and, in the army, to pull heavy guns. The hidebound British army high command rejected the idea of armored caterpillar vehicles, but when officers of the Royal Navy Air Service, who had been driving armored cars in and around air fields, picked up the idea, First Lord of the Admiralty Winston Churchill listened. Seeing the potential of a vehicle capable of climbing over trenches and barbed wire, Churchill created the "Landships Committee" on February 20, 1915. The first design prototype, "Little Willie," was tested in September 1915 and was followed in January by a larger and more practical vehicle called "Mother."

As the vehicles began to become increasingly practical, it was decided to change their name from "landships" to something more conducive to secrecy. Some authorities believe that factory workmen assembling tank hulls were told that they were building mobile water tanks for the army. Others suggest that British army lieutenant colonel Ernest Swinton simply came up with the name to use in reports to Churchill. Sir Martin Gilbert, Churchill's most authoritative biographer, reports that drawings for the vehicles were initially captioned "water carriers for Russia." Someone pointed out that this would inevitably be shortened to "WCs for Russia," *WC* being the British acronym for *water closet*: toilet. To preempt this embarrassment, the drawings were relabeled "water tanks for Russia," and from then on the name **tank** stuck. It should be noted, however, that to this day, the nomenclature of tanks retains its connection with Royal Navy origins. The underbody of the tank is a "hull," floors are "decks," internal walls or dividers are "bulkheads," and ceilings are "overheads."

Tin Can

Dating from the World War II era, this is the traditional synonym for a destroyer, which was, in that war, among the smallest and lightest of combat ships, with cramped quarters and (as sailors saw it) a special vulnerability to enemy torpedoes. These would open up a destroyer hull as readily as a can opener rips through a tin of sardines. Modern guided missile destroyers, which are much larger and more substantial vessels than their World War II ancestors, are rarely called **tin cans**; however, the phrase is often used to refer to the "designated driver" who elects to remain sober so that he may transport his or her inebriated shipmates back to vessel or base after a drunken night of liberty. The navy designation for a conventional (nonmissile) destroyer is "DD," conveniently the initials of "designated driver"—hence the modern survival and use of the phrase **tin can**.

Tits machine

What a naval aviator calls a no-nonsense, high-performance fighter jet, which is long on engine or engines but short on avionics, fly-by-wire electronics, and other modern "frills." This makes it very much a hands-on airplane, hence the "tits" designation. No supermodern aircraft—in other words, the F/A-18 Hornet—need apply. The last **tits machine** was the F-14 Tomcat and the classic was the F-8 Crusader. The F-14 was retired from the U.S. Navy in 2006, the Crusader at the end of 1999, having flown since 1959.

Torpedo (or missile) sponge

What sailors call any ship assigned to escort an aircraft carrier—point being that the true nature of the assignment is to absorb any torpedo or missile fire, thereby protecting the carrier.

USS *Slurpeefish*

Nickname for the USS *San Francisco,* a *Los Angeles*-class nuclear submarine, which bears the hull number SSN-711—the Seven-11 convenience store chain being the home of the brain-freeze-inducing Slurpee slush drink. Commissioned in 1981, SSN-711 had a high-speed collision with an undersea mountain on January 8, 2005, injuring twenty-four crewmen, one fatally. The *Slurpeefish* was nearly lost, and its skipper relieved of command. He neither sought nor was offered employment as a Seven-11 clerk.

Word shitter

An embossed label maker; frequently used in the U.S. Air Force and U.S. Navy.